CW01064536

PRAISE FOR IMMIGRIT

This research is a reflection of Ukeme's enduring spirit, lived experience as an immigrant, and professional astuteness—an important contribution to the conversation on leadership.

—Ama Marston, Co-Author,
*Type R: Transformative Resilience
for Thriving in a Turbulent World*

ImmiGRIT shines a light on the underappreciated strengths of immigrant leaders, combining Ukeme's personal journey with research and actionable advice. This timely book is a must-read for anyone seeking to foster inclusive leadership and harness the power of diverse perspectives in today's globalized world.

—Noa Ries, Co-founder, Co-ceo of Kahilla

A groundbreaking exploration of immigrant leadership, blending personal narratives with evidence-based research. Beyond its practical insights and actionable advice, ImmiGRIT is a guide for business leaders on inclusive leadership

—Eugina Jordan, CMO and Author of *Unlimited*

ImmiGRIT is pure passion, purpose, and filled with practical insights. Ukeme inspires organizations to action and empowers them with a proven system to harness the power and potential of the immigrant experience in the workplace. Leaders who put ImmiGRIT into practice will be ahead of the game and position their companies to compete better in the marketplace.

—Chris Catina, Community-first Business Strategist

True to her engineering background, Ukeme has scientifically and intelligently outlined what needs to be done and how it can be done—to harness the talents of the immigrant leaders in our midst

—Nicole Makeda, Esq., Founder Ms. Makeda Travels

Ukeme has sculpted a business masterpiece with ImmiGRIT. A well-written, easily digestible, well-researched book for every corporation that wants to benefit from the untapped and generous benefits of immigrant leadership.

—Emmanuel Olawale, Esq, Attorney and Author of
The Flavor of Favor: Quest for the American Dream

IMMIGRIT

IMMIGRIT

HOW IMMIGRANT LEADERSHIP
DRIVES BUSINESS SUCCESS

UKEME AWAKESSIEN JETER

MANUSCRIPTS PRESS

IMMIGRIT

How Immigrant Leadership Drives Business Success

ISBN   979-8-88926-064-6 *Paperback*
            979-8-88926-065-3 *Hardcover*
            979-8-88926-063-9 *Ebook*

To Aubrey and Zachary,
may your immigrant origins empower you.

—Mom

Contents

——————

FOREWORD   11

AUTHOR'S NOTE   15

INTRODUCTION   17

PART I   **25**

CHAPTER 1.   FROM IMMIGRANT TO LEADER   27

CHAPTER 2.   THE SHIFTING LANDSCAPE OF IMMIGRATION   37

CHAPTER 3.   IMMIGRATION IS SHAPING US   45

PART II   **53**

CHAPTER 4.   UNVEILING IMMIGRANTS IN DIVERSITY DISCOURSE   55

CHAPTER 5.   UNCONSCIOUS BIASES IMPACTING IMMIGRANTS   67

CHAPTER 6.   ABSENCE OF IMMIGRANT LEADERSHIP   83

CHAPTER 7.   INFLUENCE OF IMMIGRANT LEADERSHIP   95

PART III   **105**

CHAPTER 8.   UNDERSTANDING IMMIGRIT   107

CHAPTER 9.   HARNESSING IMMIGRIT   127

CHAPTER 10. CULTIVATING IMMIGRIT   149

CHAPTER 11. SUSTAINING IMMIGRIT   169

PARTING WORDS   187

ACKNOWLEDGMENTS   195

NOTES   199

WHAT'S NEXT?   221

FOREWORD

In February 2024, I received news that I had been nominated as the CMO to watch. While to many it might have seemed like just another industry recognition, it was an emotional moment for me.

As an immigrant from Russia who ventured into the world of marketing with no formal training and with English as my second language, this nomination meant everything.

To me. To my strength. To my ImmiGRIT.

Ukeme, the author of this book, coined that term. ImmiGRIT encapsulates immigrant essence as well as immigrant strength, resilience, perseverance, and resourcefulness.

Ukeme is the epitome of ImmiGRIT. She started as an engineer and then went on to get her MBA and pursued law.

And she did not stop there.

She's made history as the first BIPOC mayor in Upper Arlington, Ohio.

She's rewriting the rules, showing us all what's possible when you refuse to be boxed in by expectations.

I couldn't be prouder to call her a friend.

She's not just breaking barriers; she's smashing them to pieces, paving the way for others like her.

Like me.

Like us.

Immigrants.

It's not luck; it's ImmiGRIT.

As an immigrant, I've walked the path of navigating different cultures, languages, and perspectives in corporate America. And let me tell you, it's been a ride filled with invaluable leadership lessons.

Yet too often I've witnessed the untapped potential of immigrant leaders, including me, being overlooked in workplaces.

And this is what Ukeme's book *ImmiGRIT: How Immigrant Leadership Drives Business Success* is all about.

It's a guide for anyone who believes in the power of inclusion and wants to drive positive change in their organization.

It's a call to action, a roadmap for building a brighter, more equitable future together.

It's a manual, based on insights from immigrants and experts, that teaches how you can unleash the superpower of immigrant leadership for greater innovation and success.

Whether you're a seasoned executive or a budding professional, this book holds the keys to understanding why immigrant leadership matters and how to harness it for a brighter, more innovative future. As I reflect on my own journey, I realize that immigrant leadership isn't just a skill set. It's a force waiting to be reckoned with. You will discover the keys to unlocking this potential, fostering inclusivity, and driving innovation through these pages.

Ready to dive in?

Let's embark on a journey through this book to transform our workplaces into inclusive hubs of excellence built on understanding, empathy, and finding common ground. Through these pages, let's celebrate our shared humanity, no matter where we come from.

After all, the future of leadership is diverse, and it starts with all of us.

Companies that grasp this truth sooner rather than later are poised to survive and thrive in the ever-evolving business landscape.

Embracing diversity and immigrant voices isn't just about meeting quotas or checking boxes. It's about harnessing the full spectrum of human experience, talent, and perspective to drive innovation, creativity, and success.

So, let's lead the way together, forging a path toward a tomorrow where every voice is heard, every talent is valued, and every individual, no matter where they are born or come from, is empowered to reach their greatest potential.

With love to all of you,

Eugina Jordan, a Russian-born American, author, a CMO to watch, a mom, and a wife.

AUTHOR'S NOTE

Thank you for picking up this book. Before you begin, I have a quick note. This is a business book about conventional business topics: talent acquisition, talent development, and talent retention. As this book's title suggests, we explore the untapped power and contributions of immigrant talent, a group often marginalized and used for political warfare. I do not discuss the ethical case of immigration policies, because that hovers just beyond the pages of this book. This is simply a book about the business case and best practices for hiring, developing, and promoting immigrants to leadership.

I use the term immigrant throughout this book in its traditional meaning—to refer to persons living in a country that is not their country of birth. This population includes naturalized citizens, lawful permanent residents, refugees and asylees, persons on certain temporary visas, and unauthorized immigrants. I also use the term immigrant-origin to encompass second-generation immigrants, a group of individuals born to at least one immigrant parent. This acknowledges a group that straddles an additional layer of identity.

Before diving into this book, I want to acknowledge the immense diversity among immigrants. We are not a monolithic group. We hail from diverse places, under varied circumstances, and carry with us different privileges and socioeconomic statuses. But a unifying experience ties us together—the process of moving and establishing roots in a new country. Despite our differences, this shared journey demands a tenacity that transcends individual disparities.

Finally, I recognize that effective leadership traits are universal. In zooming in on the unique blend of leadership competencies the immigrant experience unearths, my focus on those traits does not imply exclusivity. They represent qualities shared by both immigrants and nonimmigrants. However, my emphasis on immigrants aims to further an understanding of our experiences. It seeks to illuminate the exceptional qualities that emerge from the immigrant journey and how they contribute to leadership excellence.

So, if you are a nonimmigrant perusing these pages, this book is still for you. Rest assured that the qualities discussed apply universally. Consider this an invitation to recognize the shared ground we stand on. Effective leadership knows no boundaries. Regardless of your immigrant status, the qualities discussed here do not diminish your effectiveness as a leader.

INTRODUCTION

It felt like déjà vu. I was standing outside the Alford Arena dressed in graduation regalia, observing lines of graduates streaming out. It was another graduation day at the University of Maine, my alma mater. However, this time, I was not earning another degree. I was delivering a special commencement address as a distinguished alumna at a combined graduation ceremony to the graduating classes of 2020 and 2021—the pandemic graduates.

Orono, the community where my alma mater sits, is a small town with a population of roughly ten thousand people. Over two decades had passed since I left the campus, yet everything appeared as I remembered, accompanied by a surprisingly warm breeze for a May day in Maine. As I stood there, it struck me how much this town now felt like home, considering how foreign it seemed when I arrived as an international student—where my journey as an immigrant began.

I had been invited back to deliver the commencement address in light of my recent and historic accomplishment. The milestone? In 2021, I made history as the first immigrant and person of color elected to the city council in Upper

Arlington, Ohio. In my address, I talked about my immigrant journey and encouraged the graduates to confidently go "off-script" when confronted with the twists and turns of personal and career growth. For immigrants, this call to veer off the expected path resonates deeply. Our lives, despite meticulous plans, seldom adhere to a predetermined script. In my story and the collective tales of immigrants, there's a recurring theme—the unpredictable nature of our journeys.

Standing there with my mother by my side, it all felt reminiscent of my graduation day. The only reminder that this day was new was the presence of my two children standing beside me. I congratulated the graduates as they filed out.

"Your speech was great," a mother of a graduate complimented.

I smiled and replied, "Thank you."

Another attendee remarked, "What a brave career you have had."

The compliments continued, and I sheepishly accepted them. Compliments can be awkward.

Then, a graduate approached me, thanked me for my speech, and made a comment that planted the seed for this book. "As an international student," the graduate said, "I have never considered that my immigrant experience has given me leadership skills until your speech."

I pondered those words, realizing that I had not considered this either until at least a decade into my career. Worse, many of my leaders had failed to see it too.

Immigrants have long played a vital role in shaping societies and economies worldwide, especially in America. They make significant contributions to all facets of society, including science, technology, arts, politics, and entrepreneurship. So I was shocked to discover that only 3 percent of Fortune 100 CEOs are immigrants.[1]

There is no question that more immigrants should be leading major corporations. Their experiences of leaving their homelands, adapting to new environments, and navigating unfamiliar challenges have instilled in them a remarkable ability to embrace change, overcome adversity, and think outside the box. Those are skills that make an organization profitable. Those qualities make them exceptional problem-solvers and enable them to inspire, motivate, and lead their teams to reach new heights.

Every immigrant story is nuanced and multifaceted. Yet it is often oversimplified, glorified, and reduced to a symbol of resilience or a vehicle for perpetuating the myth of the American Dream. This diminishes the complexity of the immigrant experience. Yes, resilience is a hallmark of the immigrant experience that is forged through adversity, but it also needs to be recognized as a leadership trait. Immigrants may face extraordinary challenges and overcome daunting odds, but their stories do more than inspire. Their stories showcase their leadership qualities.

IMMIGRIT

Immigrants are not a homogenous group; however, the immigrant experience has many commonalities. It unearths a unique skill set that is typically not recognized and often underutilized—a skill set that we desire in all our leaders. I have coined this skill set ImmiGRIT.

Beyond the obvious blend of "immigrant" and "grit," ImmiGRIT is ubiquitous. It encapsulates the adaptability, resilience, resourcefulness, and sheer grit exhibited by immigrants, especially immigrant women, as they navigate the complex journey of building a new life in a foreign land. The fusion of risk-taking, ingenuity, and many other advantages makes immigrants the leaders needed for the post-pandemic era.

By shifting the perception from immigrant *struggle* to immigrant *leadership*, this book lays the groundwork for a more nuanced and empowering discourse surrounding the immigrant experience. Throughout this book, the concept of ImmiGRIT is a central theme that illustrates, on the one hand, how the immigrant experience shapes individuals into remarkable leaders who enhance business growth and elevate business culture and, on the other hand, showcases how workplaces can cultivate and benefit from ImmiGRIT.

WHY THIS BOOK?

In the post-pandemic era, where globalization is a business imperative, we have a need to embrace new definitions of leadership and apply innovative approaches to teaching, learning, and developing leadership competencies. With an estimated 272 million immigrants moving about globally—surpassing some projections for 2050—and a significant increase in the number of people living in countries other than their place of birth, the landscape of talent is evolving, rapidly.[2]

In the United States alone, the immigrant population has grown by almost 30 percent between 2005 and 2022, reaching over forty-six million people and constituting 14 percent of the US population.[3] Yet many top leaders at organizations look the same, sound the same, and act the same. Nearly 90 percent of Fortune 500 CEOs are *still* White males, despite the changing demographic landscape.[4]

The absence of immigrant leadership at executive levels in corporations results in a missed opportunity that ultimately impacts profitability. Quantifying these costs precisely can be challenging due to limited research on immigrants. But what we know is that the globalization era needs the perspective of leaders who have navigated different cultures. It requires leaders who have firsthand knowledge of businesses, governments, and customers in various countries, leaders who can weigh in on topics like market expansion, evolving consumer preferences, and culture-based sales approaches. On this premise alone, the absence of immigrant leadership at the executive levels in corporations impacts profitability.

This book is personal.

When I immigrated to the United States from Nigeria at the age of eighteen to attend college, I never imagined that my immigrant experience would be more than a journey of academic pursuits; instead, it became a profound exploration of identity, resilience, and purpose. In the twenty-five years since I immigrated, I have worked in more than ten organizations, including four multibillion global companies, and not one has had an immigrant CEO.

By many accounts, I am the American Dream. For over two decades, I have navigated various leadership roles. I have worked in the private sector, in the public sector, and in specialized agencies of the United Nations. I have successfully changed careers from engineering to law. I have clenched historic political victories. I have risen to leadership ranks many only dream of. I have done so within different industries and have been celebrated for many of my achievements. *Columbus CEO* magazine has even recognized me as one of its future fifty leaders.[5]

While I have experienced many accomplishments, I have also encountered setbacks. I have led teams and I have been led. Through my experiences, I have discovered what it takes to lead immigrants to reach their fullest potential. Ultimately, the decision to write this book on leveraging immigrant leadership to drive organizational success is driven by a deeply personal understanding of the topic, illuminated by stories and research, and a genuine desire to see change. As you will discover by the end of this book, organizations led by immigrants are more profitable, more innovative, and have a better culture.

HOW THIS BOOK HELPS

While various books discuss immigration and leadership separately, this book combines these themes into a focused exploration of the specific advantages of immigrant leaders. The stories, research, and insights shared within these pages serve as a guide for business leaders on how immigrant leadership boosts business growth, supercharges company culture, and propels innovation.

This book starts a conversation on immigrant leadership. Voices of immigrants are prominently featured throughout this book, sharing personal stories, anecdotes, challenges, and triumphs. The stories humanize the immigrant experience and provide context for the strategies and recommendations outlined in this book. Additionally, this book includes expert commentary from researchers, thought leaders in immigration, and talent management.

Although this book primarily focuses on immigrant leadership, its broader message should resonate with every leader. It should inspire individuals to embrace their unique strengths and highlights an underrepresented but vital aspect of leadership.

This book is written in three parts.

> **PART 1** puts immigration in context, providing a historical view of immigration and how immigration has and is shaping us.

> **PART 2** zooms in on unique aspects of the immigrant experience that are missing in discourse on diversity, biases, and leadership.

> **PART 3** explores the tenets of ImmiGRIT and then discusses how to design and build workplace systems that unleash the full potential of ImmiGRIT.

For organizational leaders, this book illuminates the benefits of immigrant leadership and offers strategies for driving business growth through immigrant leadership. It showcases best practices for fostering an inclusive culture that effectively values and leverages immigrant talent.

For human resource professionals, talent development professionals, and diversity, equity, and inclusion professionals, this book provides actionable insights into how to support immigrant talent throughout their journey within an organization. It showcases recruitment, onboarding, career development, and retention strategies and addresses potential barriers and biases that immigrant talent may encounter. You will also find practical tips for creating inclusive policies and practices along with real-life examples of successful initiatives implemented by leading organizations.

Not least, this book is for immigrant and immigrant-origin professionals. I hope you find this book relatable and can use it to drive deeper conversations about your leadership development. This book is for all of us because we each have our part to play in building a culture inclusive of immigrant leadership.

If this book accomplishes nothing more than fostering awareness that leads to creating immigrant-informed leadership strategies, it has already justified its place on your reading list. Still, I hope this book does more than that. I hope it ushers in a new paradigm for leadership.

Let's dive in!

PART I

CHAPTER 1

FROM IMMIGRANT
TO LEADER

———

From the earliest migrations of human history to the present day, immigrants have brought a unique blend of skills that fuels progress and drives businesses forward. They have defied boundaries, shattered norms, and surpassed expectations. The transformative power of immigrants has reshaped communities, industries, and nations.

In the 1600s, British settler John Rolfe came to Virginia to develop the tobacco industry, eventually becoming the economic juggernaut that fueled the colonies' success.[1]

About a hundred years later, German immigrant Levi Strauss patented his Levi's jeans, strong metal-riveted denim trousers that were needed by the miners who ventured out west to mine and pan for gold in California.[2]

Another century later, Russian immigrant Sergey Brin cofounded Google, the revolutionary search engine that has become a verb.[3]

A quarter century later, Chinese immigrant Eric Yuan founded Zoom, a video platform that became a new verb used around the globe as the world connected with each other from their homes during a global pandemic.[4]

With rapid speed, Lebanese immigrant Noubar Afeyan codeveloped the Moderna vaccine, which helped the world open up again.[5]

These are just a few high-profile stories to illustrate a broader point. In today's globalized world—where competition is fierce, innovation is the lifeblood of progress, and change is the only constant—companies must recognize the immense value immigrants bring. In 2022, Levi's generated almost $3 billion in revenue[6] and Google generated more than $270 billion in revenue.[7]

But given the lack of visible immigrant leaders in top leadership positions across corporations today, I am convinced many leaders do not appreciate the value that immigrants bring to their organizations. Much of that stems from a lack of understanding of the immigrant journey. More aptly a lack of appreciation for the competencies that the experience unearths.

Here's mine.

FROM INTERNATIONAL STUDENT TO IMMIGRANT

Before setting foot in the United States as an eager international student, my independence was tested and refined, beginning with the intricate maze of completing college applications for a foreign education system. From figuring out transportation systems to finding housing sight unseen, every step in the process was etched with determination.

Arriving in the United States, I confronted a fresh set of complexities: adapting to an unfamiliar culture. Being an international student is like straddling two worlds, feeling foreign yet not a full-fledged immigrant either. In many ways, we are distinct from traditional immigrants, shielded from certain realities of the immigrant experience. Our purpose, after all, is singular—to pursue an education.

With roughly five hundred international students from seventy different countries, being an international student at UMaine felt like being part of a mini-United Nations, safe from the full impact of many biases. I spoke English, so language was not a barrier for me. Instead, idioms and how people used sports references in almost every conversation felt like a new language. I could follow if basketball was discussed, but I felt lost when baseball came up. I giggle now remembering the first time a classmate declared it would be a "home run" if we did an assignment a certain way. I had no idea what that meant. I was expected to know movie references to be able to laugh along in conversations and ridiculed if I had not seen a movie that was deemed as classic as American pie. I always felt overly self-conscious about my word choices and worried whether people understood me.

When it came to the classroom, I experienced a different type of culture shock. In Nigeria, the classroom experience was straightforward—listen, absorb, regurgitate. But here, I was expected to do more than just nod along. Being called upon to say anything in class was terrifying. Looking back, it probably took me a at least three years to feel comfortable raising my hand in class. Cultural adjustments to everyday living were even more complex. Whether learning how to use a vending machine for the first time or ordering food on the phone, every task felt like a crash course in cultural acrobatics.

Roughly one million international students are studying across the United States at any given time.[8] International students attend college with an F-1 visa, a class of visa that is sponsored by their school. Being an international student means being burdened with rules that native college students do not even have to think about, like having to maintain twelve credit hours each semester to be compliant with my visa while bearing in mind that auditing a class did not count toward that credit, even if I paid to audit the class; or rules like not working more than twenty hours a week.

All these rules color the international student experience, making it a markedly different experience than a native's college experience. One misstep, and the fear of being out of status looms. After graduation, international students are allowed one to three years of work experience in the US, sponsored by the school they attended. Their F-1 student visa becomes an Optional Practical Training (OPT) visa, allowing them to stay in the country *if* they have an approved job related *in* their field of study.

Because of this, the career planning support I was offered as an international student left much to be desired. It's tough to plan when you don't know what the future holds—or, more accurately, when your future depends on variables that require sponsorship by an organization or institution. My internships served a different purpose for me than those of my peers. They provided me with some context of what it felt like to work within my field. In contrast, many of my peers did internships with a dual purpose—to get experience and determine whether they wanted to work for the company they interned with. There was no holistic look at my dreams or even long-range dreams, because how could there be? Every two to three years could demand a different path, depending on your visa status and who was sponsoring you.

If international students want to stay in the US after graduating, they must apply for an H-1B work visa. To qualify for an H-1B, individuals must have proof of an education equivalent to a bachelor's degree and have a job offer from an employer who can prove that there were not any more qualified US citizen applicants interested in the position. Awkward. Then, all those applying for the H-1B visa are put into a pool and randomly selected. The US Citizenship and Immigration Services (USCIS)—the government agency that oversees immigration—selects only eighty-five thousand individuals a year to receive a H-1B visa. For the March 2022 drawing, there were 308,613 applicants for H-1B visa, according to the USCIS. Meaning only roughly 25 percent of applicants were selected.[9]

FROM IMMIGRANT TO LEADER

I was one of the lucky ones. I started my career as a mechanical engineer with my OPT, and I got selected for an H-1B when I applied. I got promoted a couple times, moving into an engineering manager role after receiving my MBA. Five years into the allotted six years of my H-1B visa, I applied to transition from my employer-sponsored H-1B visa to the sought-after permanent resident status that many know as the "green card," an immigration classification not tethered to a specific sponsor. I was advised that the waitlist was eight to eleven years. Caught between the ticking hands of time and a professional environment that failed to nurture my potential, I changed careers altogether. I went to law school to reset the immigration clock.

Being back in school meant getting back on a student visa and the opportunity to start the process again. Today, I am a lawyer, and my journey embodies resilience, adaptability, and the unwavering pursuit of personal and professional growth—each hurdle a testament to the leadership qualities forged through being an immigrant.

Attending law school was a significant sacrifice, but it became a strategic move to maintain a viable immigration status. The subsequent years were marked by late nights of studying, juggling legal internships, entering motherhood, and adapting to a new professional identity. As I reflect on my journey, I see the challenges I faced and the triumphs I achieved.

Adapting to new environments, overcoming bureaucratic hurdles, and navigating the immigration processes demanded unwavering perseverance.

Adapting to new environments, overcoming bureaucratic hurdles, and navigating the immigration processes demanded unwavering perseverance. Having worked in corporations, served in public office, built and led communities, and led teams, I've consistently witnessed how my experience as an immigrant makes me a better leader. Now, as a history maker, I am celebrated as achieving the American Dream.

A common question people always ask me is, "How did you do it?" I usually find myself responding, "Because I am an immigrant." Being an immigrant feels like my superpower. Being an immigrant gives me a distinct perspective that bolsters me in the most challenging situations. Despite living in an era where diversity and inclusion are championed, I still frequently find myself being the only immigrant leader in many rooms. And, as an immigrant, I often feel left out of the diversity and inclusion lens altogether.

There is no single pathway or common formula for ascending to leadership, yet the visible lack of immigrant leaders in senior leadership positions signals a problem. The encounter I had with the graduating international student who approached me after my commencement speech has left me with the impression that business leaders are failing to leverage immigrant leadership.

THE INFLUENCE OF MY FIRST LEADER—JOEY

I started my career in manufacturing. My introduction to the professional world was influenced by Joey, a leader whose impact has reverberated throughout my career. As the superintendent for converting, Joey oversaw half of the entire operations for the manufacturing plant. What made Joey's influence stand out even more to me was that he was my skip-level leader, not my direct report boss, so I only had official meetings with him about once a month. However, we would see each other around the plant, and each time he would use the opportunity to check in and share a resource with me to advance a project I was working on. His impact on me was so immense, it became the standard against which I have measured every subsequent leader.

One of my fondest encounters with Joey was discussing my work visa. I started with the company on my OPT visa, which was sponsored by UMaine, and I needed a plan to transition it to a H-1B visa when my OPT came to an end. Joey had never heard of the process before, so he had never guided an employee through it. But he committed himself to learning and supporting my needs so I could achieve my full potential in my career. Ultimately, with Joey's advocacy, the company decided to become the sponsor for my H-1B visa.

Even two decades later, I have maintained a connection with Joey, a testament to the enduring influence of a remarkable leader. Curious about the secrets behind Joey's exemplary leadership, I reached out to him for insights on his leadership philosophy. His response was refreshingly simple yet profoundly impactful—active listening.

Joey went on to explain that it's about truly hearing what people have to say, what they have been through, and what they are going through. It's about understanding their feelings and experiences in the workplace and making them feel valued and included. He believes that when a leader actively listens, they acknowledge the presence and contributions of their team members, thereby fostering a sense of belonging and worth. Even if their roles may not be the most glamorous, taking the time to listen makes them feel like they're an integral part of the team, not just relegated to the sidelines.

Under Joey's guidance, our manufacturing facility achieved numerous accolades, including recognition for productivity, safety performance, and efficiency in machine changeovers. Meanwhile, some high visibility assignments got me promoted in two short years, and as they say, the rest is history.

We need more Joeys in the workplace, which is why I have written this book. Leaders hold the power to harness immigrant leadership in driving organizational success. While political rhetoric often clouds the immigration narrative, we need leaders who recognize the wonder, doubt, joy, fear, and self-discovery accompanying how immigrants find and define their space in the new world.

CHAPTER 2

THE SHIFTING LANDSCAPE OF IMMIGRATION

———

Globally, the US is home to more immigrants than any other country in the world. While the US population represents only about 5 percent of the total world population, nearly 20 percent of all global migrants reside in the US.[1]

Since its inception, the US has been a beacon for those seeking new beginnings. From the colonial period through the Industrial Revolution and the Great Depression, the US population has been shaped by radical shifts in immigration policies. Remarkably, immigration was among the earliest challenges faced by American politicians when determining the criteria for citizenship. While the Constitution enumerates powers, the Founding Fathers did not explicitly address immigration as one of these powers.

The roots of immigration in America traces back to its very founding.

In 1620, around one hundred individuals, later known as the Pilgrims, sought refuge in present-day Plymouth,

Massachusetts, fleeing religious persecution in Europe.[2] Simultaneously, many others arrived in pursuit of economic opportunities before a tragic chapter unfolded as enslaved people from West Africa were brought to America against their will during the colonial period.

The first major wave of immigrants occurred between 1815 and 1865 with a majority of the immigrants originating from northern and western Europe.[3] Notably, Irish immigrants, escaping a devastating famine in the mid-nineteenth century, formed a significant portion of that wave. Cities along America's East Coast witnessed their settlement. Subsequently, in the late nineteenth century, a surge of five million German immigrants sought refuge in the US, impacting cities like Milwaukee, St. Louis, and Cincinnati.[4] These waves of migration collectively contributed to the enduring characterization of America as the land of immigrants.

For generations, immigrants have arrived with boundless hopes and dreams, fueled by the notion that American streets were metaphorically paved with gold. While not necessarily referring to material wealth, this belief encapsulates the opportunity that awaited future generations.

The term *American Dream* was popularized in 1931 by James Truslow Adams, an American writer and historian.[5] He established it as:

> That dream of a land in which life should be better and richer and fuller for everyone, with opportunity for each according to ability or achievement... It is not a dream of motor cars and high wages merely, but a dream of social order in which each man and each woman shall be able

to attain to the fullest stature… and be recognized by others for what they are, regardless of the fortuitous circumstances of birth or position.

Adams envisioned a life where everyone could experience richness and fulfillment with opportunities available based on ability and achievement, irrespective of social class or circumstances of birth. The American Dream, a phrase echoing through the corridors of history, encapsulates a collective ethos in the US. This set of ideals carries diverse meanings for different individuals and universally implies the promise of prosperity through diligence. At its core, the American Dream embodies equality, justice, democracy, and the freedom for individuals to attain prosperity and success. It signifies upward social mobility for oneself and future generations, achievable through hard work.

Without turning this portion of the book into a history lesson, it is important to demonstrate how immigration and the policies enacted have evolved to give you deeper context into how immigration has impacted the US. Immigration policy debates involve a delicate balance between economic, geopolitical, and humanitarian concerns. However, these discussions sometimes mask underlying racial biases, diverting attention from the core issues.

IMMIGRATION BEFORE 1965: A TINGED HISTORY

The first set of American immigration laws were crafted with the explicit aim of preserving a White population. Those laws favored individuals of European descent from northern and western European regions and rejected groups like Italians and Jews.[6] Rooted in racism and the belief in the superiority of certain genetic traits, these biases continued to influence policies. As the definition of *Whiteness* evolved and amendments in laws were made, remnants of earlier biases persisted.[7]

> *To call America a nation of immigrants is not wrong, but it coexists with the reality that the country's immigration system has never been color-blind.*

Congress passed the Naturalization Act of 1790, extending citizenship to "free White persons of good character."[8] The law excluded indentured servants, nonwhites, and enslaved people from naturalization. However, Congress lacked an enumerated power under the Constitution to control immigration, so they found a way around this by creating laws that limited how many people could travel on a ship coming to America. In 1819, Congress indirectly regulated immigration under the guise of safety by limiting the number of passengers a ship could carry.[9] This legislation lowered the carrying capacity of passenger ships and increased the price of travel, consequently reducing the number of *poor* immigrants.

The mid-nineteenth century marked the arrival of Chinese immigrants. Their success in the agricultural industry fueled anti-Chinese sentiment, particularly in California, leading to the Chinese Exclusion Act of 1882, which restricted future Chinese immigration to the US.[10] This Act was a watershed moment in American immigration policy as the first significant federal legislation restricting immigration. Initially imposing a ten-year ban on Chinese laborers, Congress later extended this ban through 1943—a whopping sixty-one years of total ban.

Throughout much of the 1800s, immigration was regulated by individual states. In the final decade of the century, the federal government recognized the need to manage the escalating influx of newcomers. So, in 1890, President Benjamin Harrison designated Ellis Island, situated in New York Harbor near the Statue of Liberty, as the federal immigration station. The station opened on January 1, 1892, welcoming a record number of nearly 450,000 people in its inaugural year. By its closure in 1954, an estimated twelve million individuals had passed through the island.[11]

IMMIGRATION BETWEEN 1880–1920: AN ERA OF RAPID CHANGE

Between 1880 and 1920, over twenty million immigrants arrived in America.[12] Predominantly hailing from central, eastern, and southern Europe, this wave included over two million Jews who were fleeing religious persecution from Eastern Europe.[13]

From 1890 through 1920, the federal government enacted several immigration acts that expanded inadmissible classes of immigrants, increased deportation powers, and raised the head tax on immigrants.[14] The Immigration Act of 1924 enacted a quota system, favoring immigrants from Western Europe and restricting entry to 2 percent of the total number of people of other nationalities while still explicitly prohibiting immigrants from Asia.[15]

The global depression of the 1930s and World War II led to a substantial decrease in immigration. Between 1930 and

1950, the American foreign-born population declined from 14.2 million to 10.3 million.[16] Post-war, Congress enacted special legislation allowing *only* refugees from Europe and the Soviet Union to enter the US, again maintaining the Whiteness of allowed immigrants.

Before 1921, immigration laws primarily focused on excluding immigrants based on their origins and allowing migration for individuals not explicitly excluded. Post-1921 and what still persists today, immigration laws have shifted to deciding *which* immigrants to admit. Though no longer based on race, this favoritism leans toward those with financial means, education, and skills while restricting entry for those not meeting those specific criteria.

IMMIGRATION POST-1965: A TRANSFORMATIVE ERA

Standing before Congress on January 8, 1964, President Lyndon B. Johnson delivered his State of the Union Address. In this address, he called for the abolition of racial discrimination, foreshadowing the Civil Rights Act's passage later that year.[17] The push to eliminate racially motivated quotas extended to immigration laws, and subsequently, the Immigration and Nationality Act of 1965 was born.

The Immigration and Nationality Act of 1965 dismantled the racially biased national origin quotas established in the 1920s. The quota system was replaced with a preference system, emphasizing family reunification and skilled immigrants. Upon signing the bill, President Lyndon B. Johnson condemned the old immigration system as "un-American," pledging that the new legislation would correct a "cruel and enduring wrong in the conduct of the American Nation."[18]

The past half-century has witnessed a transformative wave of immigration in the US, distinct in ethnicity, education, and occupation from previous eras. Immigrants now constitute almost 14 percent of the US population, marking a fourfold increase since 1960.[19] This diverse population, representing nearly every country globally, is projected to contribute significantly to the US's population growth through 2065.[20]

WHERE IMMIGRATION STANDS TODAY

The debate surrounding immigration is woven with moral and economic threads. Advocates for liberal immigration policies invoke the iconic phrase on the Statue of Liberty, *"Give me your tired, your poor, your huddled masses,"* emphasizing America's humanitarian imperative to provide refuge and opportunities for those seeking a better life. Economically, they argue that immigrants contribute to innovation and growth through diverse skills and entrepreneurial endeavors, fostering a dynamic workforce.

Opponents of liberal immigration policies express apprehensions about job competition and strains on public resources. Central to their concerns is the fear of creating a lasting underclass of unassimilated families. They argue that an influx of immigrants from economically disadvantaged backgrounds may hinder social assimilation, economic mobility, and educational opportunities.

Critics propose a more selective approach, favoring individuals with higher skills or economic means. By targeting restrictions on entry for those with lower socioeconomic status, proponents of tighter controls aim to balance preserving job opportunities for native citizens and ensuring effective assimilation. But authors Abramitzky and Boustan challenge that approach in their book titled *Streets of Gold: America's Untold Story of Immigrant Success.* The authors point to historical events, like the Mariel boatlift, to illustrate that low-skill immigrants historically filled jobs that would otherwise be unfilled or automated.[21] In areas with high immigration, businesses have access to more workers, reducing the incentive for further automation.

It is clear that immigrants have been instrumental in developing America's demographic make-up and status as a global leader in commerce. It's the secret sauce of America, the land of immigrants. Today's America continues to build on past successes. In the next chapter we will uncover how immigration is shaping us.

CHAPTER 3

IMMIGRATION IS SHAPING US

———

When you hear the word *immigrant*, who do you picture? Do you imagine physical attributes? Perhaps you imagine someone speaking with an accent. It may even invoke an image of a person crossing the border.

The classic stereotype of immigrants, especially in America, is one of penniless individuals working low-paying jobs, aiming to achieve parity in skills and income with natives. Immigrant success stories are frequently coined as the American Dream. They are portrayed as stories that can only happen in America—the land of opportunity. But there's a problem with stereotypes. In her TEDx talk titled, "The Danger of a Single Story," Nigerian writer Chimamanda Adichie warns that, "The problem with stereotypes is not that they are not true, but they are incomplete...they make one story become the only story."[1]

Blaming immigrants for the nation's woes has long been an American pastime, especially during challenging economic times. At the time of writing this book, there is an upsurge in anti-immigrant sentiment, particularly in areas of the US that host large numbers of immigrants. Misconceptions about immigration and how the system works coupled with divisive political rhetoric have complicated the discourse around immigration. Default assumptions, conclusions, and decisions stoke fear and misunderstanding, hindering a more complex, nuanced view of immigration. This robs immigrants of their dignity.

One of the most well-entrenched myths about immigrants is that they steal jobs from American workers, collect an excess of government benefits, and, in general, represent a drain on the economy. But these myths must be refuted to create a more hospitable workplace for immigrants. The truth is, immigration is shaping us.

Immigrants have shaped American democracy, constructed its infrastructure, and propelled it into the world's greatest economy brick by brick and invention by invention.

IMMIGRATION IS SHAPING POPULATION

Countries are facing a demographic dilemma around the globe. From Asia to Europe, the workforce is aging, and birthrates are on a downward trajectory. As we saw in chapter 2, few transformations have left a more indelible mark on the racial landscape of America than the past five decades of immigration. In the not-so-distant past, racial discourse primarily revolved around the dichotomy of Black and White. Rewind to 1960, and you'll find a staggering 85 percent of Americans identifying as White. Back then, when the term "minorities" was uttered, it typically referred to Black individuals.

However, the tide of immigration has ushered in a new era, reshaping both the demographic composition of the nation and the very notions we hold about race. Moreover, immigration has spurred the evolution of our racial lexicon, introducing new terms and categories that reflect the diverse tapestry of American society. The designation "Hispanic," for instance, was virtually nonexistent half a century ago but has since become a pervasive descriptor, embraced not only by those of Latin American descent but also by non-Hispanics seeking to encapsulate the cultural and ethnic diversity of the Hispanic community. Similarly, terms like "Latino" and the more gender-inclusive "Latinx" have gained traction, further enriching our discourse on race and identity.

In 2021, the US witnessed fewer than one million in population growth.[2] For the first time since 1937 the country has experienced the lowest numeric growth.[3] Despite this decline in population growth, the US has seen substantial growth in its racial and ethnic minority populations over the past few decades. Non-Hispanic Whites remain the largest racial group, but their share of the total population has gradually declined. Hispanics, Asians, African Americans, and other ethnic groups have witnessed an increase in numbers, contributing to a more racially and ethnically diverse population in the US.[4]

- Hispanic Population Growth: The Hispanic population in the US has witnessed substantial growth fueled by immigration and higher birthrates. Now the largest minority group in the country, Hispanics are projected to continue their upward trajectory.
- Asian Population Growth: Similarly, the Asian American population has experienced significant expansion,

driven by immigration, high birthrates, and an influx of international students and skilled workers from Asian countries.

- African American Population Growth: The African American population has steadily grown, albeit slightly slower than other minority groups. Contributing factors include natural increase and migration patterns.
- Multiracial Identity Population Growth: A growing number of Americans now identify as multiracial, reflecting the increasing complexity of racial identity. This shift mirrors changing demographics and greater societal acceptance of mixed-race identities.

The year 2030 is slated to be a demographic turning point for the US, as highlighted in a research report on population estimates and projections by the US Census Bureau.[5] From that year onward, all baby boomers will be older than 65, constituting one in every five Americans projected to be of retirement age.

Additionally, 2030 marks another demographic first for the US, where due to population aging, immigration is projected to surpass natural increase as the primary driver of population growth.[6] The evolving population of the US is a multifaceted and ongoing process shaped by immigration, birthrates, aging, and diversity; however, it is primarily shaped by immigration. These demographic changes carry far-reaching implications for the country's economy, society, and politics.

IMMIGRATION IS SHAPING THE ECONOMY
Beyond shaping the demographic landscape, immigration profoundly influences economic dynamics. Immigration

has catalyzed innovation, driven growth, and shaped entire industries. Immigrants are credited with practically inventing Silicon Valley and have played a significant role in the high-tech sector, now a cornerstone of the American economy.

Insights from the *Global Entrepreneurship Monitor 2012 Global Report* shows that immigrants are more inclined toward entrepreneurial endeavors.[7] And not just in the United States but across sixty-nine countries. Immigrants are why 23 percent of patents were issued between 1990 and 2016, contributing not just in quantity but also in the quality and utility of patents.[8] They were responsible for a quarter of the total economic value of patents, as measured by the stock market's reaction.[9]

In 2018, over half of the ninety-one US start-up companies valued at $1 billion or more had at least one immigrant founder, highlighting immigrants' entrepreneurial spirit and contributions to the economy. Immigrants are twice as likely to venture into entrepreneurship compared to their US-born counterparts, constituting an impressive 27.5 percent of US entrepreneurs.[10] Furthermore, immigrants make up a substantial portion of business owners nationwide.

Immigrants have also played a critical role in sustaining various service industries, filling essential roles across all occupational levels—from agriculture to healthcare. Notably, many physicians, surgeons, and registered nurses in the United States are immigrants, addressing shortages in critical healthcare professions. As companies are fiercely competing for the best talent amid a global shortage, other countries are actively attracting immigrants to remain competitive. For instance, Canada recently announced open work permits for US work visa holders[11] while Britain created the High Potential Visa to attract graduates from predominantly US schools.[12] Australia, Germany, and other nations are following suit.

Contrary to concerns about native workers being negatively impacted by immigration, research suggests otherwise. American corporations are actually at risk of losing their competitive edge with the global talent shortage. Economists say immigration has had minimal adverse effects on wages and employment for native-born workers. In fact, immigrants contribute to increased demand for goods and services, and immigrant-owned small businesses often create opportunities for native-born workers. Immigrants contribute to consumer spending and tax revenue, further stimulating economic growth. As consumers, they purchase goods and services, supporting local businesses and contributing to overall demand. Additionally, immigrants pay taxes, including income taxes, property taxes, and sales taxes, which fund public services and infrastructure.

Overall, immigrants have a positive fiscal impact on the US economy, with their contributions outweighing the costs associated with public services and benefits.

IMMIGRATION IS SHAPING CULTURE

Immigrants are not only reshaping but invigorating what we consider to be quintessentially American culture. They bring with them rich traditions, flavors, and perspectives that have profoundly influenced the foods we savor, the music we groove to, the films we eagerly anticipate, and the literature that captures our imaginations.

Think back to the culinary landscape of America. While bagels and pizza may have been introduced by Jewish and Italian immigrants respectively, today, salsa outsells ketchup, and tacos have become a staple in American cuisine.[13] In fact, Chinese restaurants in the US outnumber all the fast-food giants combined, offering a diverse array of regional dishes and flavors that tantalize our taste buds. Immigrant communities have become epicenters of culinary innovation, blending traditional recipes with local ingredients to create gastronomic delights that reflect the diversity of American society.

Beyond the culinary realm, immigrants and their descendants have made significant contributions to literature, with many new authors of immigrant descent gracing bestseller lists. Their works explore timeless immigrant themes, such as cultural adaptation, and shed light on contemporary issues like undocumented status, offering nuanced perspectives that resonate with readers across the nation.

Immigrants are leaving an indelible mark on the entertainment industry, with a growing number of stars, writers, and producers of immigrant or immigrant-origin making waves in film, music, and television. These individuals bring fresh perspectives and narratives to the screen, enriching our cultural landscape with stories that reflect the complexities of the immigrant experience in America. They redefine popular music, infusing rhythms and melodies like afro beats into mainstream genres while creating a fusion of sounds that captivates audiences worldwide. Pop music superstars with roots in Latin America have propelled Latin music to the forefront of the music industry, showcasing the richness and diversity of Hispanic culture while simultaneously bridging cultural divides and uniting audiences through the universal language of music.

Immigrants and their descendants have broadened the horizons of mainstream American culture and pioneered new artistic expressions that seamlessly blend elements of American and immigrant cultures. Their creative contributions are a testament to the transformative power of diversity, enriching our collective experience and reinforcing the notion that cultural exchange is the heartbeat of a vibrant and inclusive society.

* * *

The story of immigration and its impact isn't about one country or one policy; it's about a global shift in demographics, economies, and societies.

While I have focused on the US, governments around the globe are grappling with the challenges of maintaining a vibrant and productive workforce amid aging populations and declining birthrates.

PART II

CHAPTER 4

UNVEILING IMMIGRANTS IN DIVERSITY DISCOURSE

I was shocked when I asked a senior diversity leader of a major US corporation how many immigrants their organization had in senior leadership—meaning director level or higher—and the response was, "We don't track that." While the shock of this revelation lingered, it became apparent that such a lack of tracking was not an isolated case. Throughout my research for this book, I engaged with numerous human resource professionals across organizations of different sizes, and not a single one practiced self-identification or self-reporting of employees' immigrant status.

How can this be? Organizations interested in succeeding in their diversity and inclusion initiatives must take an honest, fact-based approach to understand where they fall short.

Immigration goes beyond being a simple economic activity. It profoundly contributes to cultural vibrancy and diversity. Integrating diverse cultural perspectives within organizations is a cornerstone for cultivating dynamic and inclusive leadership structures, providing a distinctive competitive advantage to firms. In navigating the complexities of today's dynamic landscape, effective leadership requires intentionally cultivating diverse perspectives and fostering complex thinking capabilities.

The organizational advantages stemming from diversity have been thoroughly documented since the early 1990s. Numerous articles and research studies explore best practices for organizations to cultivate an environment and culture that champion diversity, equity, and inclusion (DEI), emphasizing the value of diverse perspectives and individuals. However, the intent of this book diverges from that well-trodden path. This chapter deliberately narrows its focus to scrutinize how our DEI efforts currently fall short in comprehensively incorporating immigrants and delineates the necessary steps for transformative change.

UNDERSTANDING INTERSECTIONALITY

January 2000 was my first Dr. Martin Luther King, Jr. (MLK) holiday in America. Because it was a long weekend, many students had gone home, and the campus was desolate. Unable to return home to Port Harcourt, Nigeria, *just* for the weekend, I stayed on campus.

While strolling across campus on MLK Day to meet up with another international student, I was approached by a news reporter. "Can we interview you?" they inquired.

Without hesitating or seeking clarity on the subject, I responded, "Yes," an impulsive decision that would soon reveal itself as a mistake.

The reporter asked, "What does the legacy of Dr. Martin Luther King, Jr. mean to you?"

A sudden sense of pressure enveloped me. I momentarily froze, my mouth agape, struggling to articulate a response. Subconsciously aware that my initial thoughts might not be suitable for the camera, I hesitated. As the reporter motioned for an answer, I blurted out, "I'm from Nigeria!" Panicking, I added, "But I know who Dr. Martin Luther King is."

As awkward as that day was, it dawned on me that, as a Black individual in America, I felt compelled to justify my knowledge of MLK, perhaps due to societal expectations or assumptions. The encounter highlighted the complexity of identity and expectations, showcasing the subtle pressures of navigating conversations about race and culture, even on a day commemorating a pivotal figure like MLK.

Over three decades have passed since Kimberlé Crenshaw introduced the term "intersectionality" to illuminate how discrimination against various facets of a person's identity can overlap and significantly impact their lives.[1] Crenshaw's groundbreaking 1989 work titled "Demarginalizing the Intersection of Race and Sex" emphasized that intersectional experience transcends the sum of racism and sexism. Any analysis that neglects intersectionality falls short of addressing the unique subordination Black women face.

While Crenshaw initially focused on the intersectionality of Black women, the concept encompassed the intertwining complexities of factors such as skin color, gender, disability, sexual orientation, accent, and cultural heritage. It acknowledges that these facets interact, contributing to unequal outcomes that cannot be attributed to one dimension alone.

The repercussions of intersectionality are palpable in the workplace, where individuals belonging to two or more underrepresented categories experience oppression and limited opportunities in distinct ways. Recognizing the power of intersectionality in immigrant leadership is pivotal for shaping the future of successful corporations.

A fundamental aspect of intersectionality is acknowledging how multiple social, cultural, and personal identities intersect. Immigrants, in particular, carry layers of identity beyond their national origin. These may include ethnicity, race, gender, religion, and language.

Ethnicity, for instance, connects people through shared cultural characteristics like customs, language, and food. In the US, diverse ethnic communities have thrived since the first wave of immigrants—from Dutch-origin communities in central Pennsylvania to Swedish-heritage neighborhoods outside Chicago as well as the Haitians and Cuban-American enclave in Miami, among many others.

Understanding and embracing this richness of identity is critical for developing leadership processes that resonate with immigrant communities' diverse experiences. Navigating the intersectionality of immigrants requires a nuanced approach beyond superficial categorizations, acknowledging the unique challenges and strengths each individual brings to the table.

As we strive to create effective leadership processes, incorporating the principles of intersectionality ensures that our strategies are inclusive and comprehensive. By recognizing the complexity of individuals' identities, we pave the way for more equitable, diverse, and successful leadership in the ever-evolving landscape of our globalized world.

Ethnicity shapes our experiences, offering unique perspectives that supplement our views on workplaces and meetings, making them more robust and inclusive. This diversity of perspectives is a valuable asset that enriches our collective understanding.

Another concept related to ethnicity is nationality, sometimes called country of origin or national origin. These terms—encompassing attributes such as birthplace, ethnicity, ancestry, culture, and language—are used interchangeably in the US. It's important to distinguish these concepts from an individual's race.

We must understand that individuals, regardless of their ethnicity, nationality, or country of origin, can make valuable contributions. This emphasis on understanding intersectionality allows us to appreciate the complexity of individual identities and the unique strengths they bring to the table.

The intersectionality of immigration and DEI efforts represents a complex interplay influencing the dynamics of societies and organizations. Understanding and navigating this intersection is vital for fostering inclusive environments.

COMPLICATED INTERSECTION OF IMMIGRATION AND DEI EFFORTS

Recognition of intersectionality facilitates the development of inclusive policies and practices tailored to address the unique needs and challenges immigrants face while ensuring equitable access to opportunities and contributing to the overall success of DEI initiatives.

Some immigrants face more challenges than others, reflecting the diversity of the immigrant experience and the compounding impacts of intersectional factors such as immigration status, race and ethnicity, and income. Black and Hispanic immigrants, likely undocumented immigrants, immigrants with limited English proficiency, and lower-income immigrants, face disproportionate challenges given the impacts of racism, fears, and uncertainties related to immigration status, language barriers, and financial challenges.[2]

Navigating the complexities of immigration demands a nuanced approach, balancing inclusivity with adherence to existing DEI frameworks. Language differences, for example, may challenge effective communication within DEI efforts, highlighting the importance of overcoming linguistic barriers for accessibility.

Achieving cultural sensitivity is an ongoing challenge, requiring continuous efforts to prevent the unintentional perpetuation of stereotypes or biases. An intersectional approach is essential to address biases related to various facets of diversity, especially as immigrants face intersectional discrimination. Later in this book, we explore some of the biases distinctive to immigrants.

Economic disparities often intersect with immigration challenges, demanding efforts to address these disparities and ensure economic opportunities are accessible to all, regardless of background. Immigration status can impact access to resources such as education, healthcare, and social services, requiring consideration and action within DEI initiatives to ensure equitable access.

Resistance to immigrant-inclusive DEI efforts may exist in the workplace, emphasizing the need for education, dialogue, and shared understanding of the benefits that diversity, including immigration, brings. Advocating for policies that support immigration within DEI frameworks becomes key in fostering a supportive and inclusive workplace.

The intricate relationship between immigration and DEI efforts offers both richness and challenges. Successfully navigating this intersection demands sustained commitment, awareness, and strategic approaches to foster inclusivity and equity within organizations.

WHY DEI EFFORTS SHOULD TRACK IMMIGRANTS

Recognizing and tracking immigrants within DEI initiatives is important for fostering a diverse and representative organizational landscape. Including immigrants at all levels, especially in senior leadership roles, contributes to a more comprehensive representation of diverse perspectives and experiences within the company.

This practice aligns with the principles of equitable opportunities, as tracking immigrant demographics allows organizations to assess and address potential barriers hindering their career advancement. By understanding the composition of senior leadership, companies can identify and rectify biases or systemic issues that may impede the professional growth of immigrant employees.

Furthermore, tracking immigrants facilitates the implementation of targeted support programs. These initiatives can address immigrants' unique challenges, such as cultural adjustment, language barriers, and specific career development needs. Tailoring support programs contributes to a more inclusive and supportive workplace environment.

Accurate and comprehensive diversity data reflect a commitment to transparency and accountability in DEI efforts. Moreover, tracking immigrants enhances cultural competence within the workplace. Understanding immigrant employees' unique experiences and perspectives fosters an environment that embraces diversity, creates a sense of belonging, and contributes to overall employee satisfaction and engagement.

In a broader context, tracking immigrants in leadership roles aligns with strategic decision-making. It empowers leaders to make informed choices, leveraging immigrant employees' diverse skills, perspectives, and experiences. This strategic approach drives innovation and positions organizations competitively in a globalized and diverse marketplace.

Identifying and tracking immigrants in DEI efforts is foundational for creating an inclusive workplace that values diversity, ensures equitable opportunities, and strategically positions organizations for success in an interconnected and diverse world. Organizations can leverage information such as self-identification to allocate resources and support to candidates within an underrepresented category. The information can impact access to benefits, training, and mentorship. Leaders can also use data to help launch or expand DEI initiatives that can help enhance employee engagement and aid in retention efforts.

Many people, especially those who belong to marginalized groups, can be hesitant to reveal their identities. A key component to successful self-identification is transparent communication. Letting employees know that their information remains confidential, their identities matter, and their voluntary self-identification helps can ensure that resources are more equitably allocated and can help increase participation in surveys. To further alleviate concerns, it's important to let people know how to submit their information, where it will be stored, who has access, how the company plans to use data, and what initiatives have been established as a result of previous self-identification campaigns.

Globally sourcing data poses considerable challenges for companies, stemming from many factors, including diverse country regulations, unfamiliarity with culturally nuanced dimensions of diversity, and the lasting impact of historical events on laws, norms, and individuals' comfort levels in sharing demographic information. For example, Germany and France bear the weight of caution ingrained in their approach to collecting ethnicity data, a caution rooted in the use of population registries and identity cards during World War II and the Holocaust. Such historical echoes persist, shaping present-day attitudes on identification.

The variance in acceptable terms further complicates the global data collection landscape. For instance, in Sweden, the term "race" is eschewed, replaced by more encompassing and culturally sensitive alternatives, "ethnic origin" or "foreign origin."[3] Germany grapples with the dual meaning of "Rasse," which translates to both "race" and "breed" for animals, prompting ongoing debates regarding the removal of the term "race" from the constitutional lexicon.[4]

Navigating the European Union adds an additional layer of complexity, as collecting ethnicity data requires explicit consent from employees or anonymization of the data.[5] Stricter regulations highlight the cautious approach to respecting individual privacy and mitigating potential biases.

Furthermore, legal and cultural constraints in certain countries pose obstacles to voluntary information disclosure. For instance, collecting sexual identity data faces resistance in countries with laws against homosexuality, while gathering religious data encounters challenges in regions where religious minorities regularly contend with bias. The interplay of legal frameworks, cultural norms, and historical legacies are just some of the complexities that companies must navigate when embarking on global data collection endeavors.

However, these challenges should not prevent companies from asking employees to self-identify when possible. Self-identification, particularly through open-ended questions, can help in these instances by enabling people to claim their identities in a way that acknowledges regulation and privacy concerns.

UNLOCKING THE POWER OF IMMIGRANT LEADERSHIP FOR DIVERSITY

Immigrant leadership can play a pivotal role in cultivating diversity within organizations. Immigrants, enriched by their diverse backgrounds and life experiences, bring a wealth of unique skills and perspectives that profoundly shape corporate strategies, decision-making processes, and overall organizational dynamics. By embodying a blend of cultural influences, immigrant leaders offer invaluable global insights essential for navigating the complexities of our interconnected world and effectively addressing the diverse needs of both the workforce and customers.

The distinct experiences of immigrant leaders fuel a rich diversity of thought that translate into creative problem-solving and innovative thinking as well as innovative approaches and solutions. These contribute to increased revenue, a culture of continuous improvement, and adaptability within organizations.

Including immigrant leaders in decision-making creates more comprehensive, adaptive, and innovative leadership teams. Organizations that embrace and leverage the unique qualities of immigrant leaders not only navigate the challenges of a globalized world more effectively but also foster a work culture that thrives on diversity. This phenomenon, recognized as an essential aspect of inclusive leadership, embraces the richness of different cultures, backgrounds, and ideas.

Changing the face of leadership is everybody's job. If you are an existing leader, your decisions about hiring, promoting, and shaping the leadership teams matter.

CHAPTER 5

UNCONSCIOUS BIASES IMPACTING IMMIGRANTS

Unconscious biases play a significant role in shaping attitudes, actions, and decisions. These biases, often based on social stereotypes, are unintentional, automatic, and deeply ingrained in the subconscious. Immigrants face unique unconscious biases due to cultural differences and preconceived notions. Recognizing and addressing these unconscious biases is essential in creating workplaces that allow immigrant leaders to thrive.

Immigrants of color, in particular, are treated as scapegoats for the country's immigration problems, particularly during times of economic unrest. Consequently, they are the ones most impacted by unconscious biases. Political leaders often utilize anti-immigrant rhetoric, whether explicitly or implicitly, as a way to "other" immigrants. Whether conscious or unconscious, explicit or implicit, negative characterizations and descriptions of immigrants have a trickle-down effect that shape our perceptions and treatment of immigrants in the workplace, beginning from the recruiting process up to excluding them from leadership opportunities.

When I returned to the University of Maine (UMaine) to deliver my commencement speech, I was introduced to Anila Karunakar, the director of Multicultural Programs. I did not remember this role existing when I attended UMaine, so I was immediately curious. Anila explained it as a role within the division of student affairs focused on leading and strengthening the advocacy and support for multicultural, multiethnic students and marginalized communities on campus. Naturally, the next thing I had to know was how she got to UMaine.

I was drawn to Anila's vibrant personality and was not the only one, judging from the stream of students who dropped by her office when I was conversing with her. With her hair pulled back in a loose bun that showed off her beautiful gold earrings, she wore a traditional Indian outfit that I learned was a salwar kameez. Hers was emerald green with intricate gold embroidery. Her office was plastered with art from different countries, pictures from her travels, and posters with affirming messages supporting various communities— from indigenous people to LGBTQ+.

Anila grew up as an immigrant her entire life, first as an Indian raised in Bahrain and then as an Indian in America. She told me, "My journey to America was not my choice, but rather a result of my parents' decision." Initially, Anila had no desire to come to the US. She wanted to return to her home country of India and felt confident about her opportunities there. However, her parents believed studying in the US would benefit her, and she agreed.

We bonded over our initial struggles and the difficulties faced as international students in a small town—hers in Orange City, Iowa, and me in Orono, Maine—where people had little knowledge about our backgrounds and cultures.

She laughed, remembering, "Nobody in Iowa seems to know where Bahrain is, where India is... I would get asked all the time whether Bahrain is part of India." In case you're curious too, Bahrain is an island country in the Middle East situated in a bay on the southwestern coast of the Persian Gulf. Its name is from the Arabic term al-baḥrayn, meaning "two seas."

Becoming the immigrant leader she is today, Anila had to navigate code-switching, downplaying her cultural identity, and conforming to Western norms of leadership. Pressure mounted to be more palatable and assimilate to increase her chances of being chosen for leadership positions.

Anila recalls how she embarked on her leadership journey. During her sophomore year in college, her peers elected her as the president of the international club. She shared with me the circumstances surrounding her selection, revealing that she was picked over her peers, including those of Japanese and Korean descent, who she perceived as smarter than her due to their dual majors.

Anila couldn't help but notice the difference that led to her selection. She said, "The reason I was chosen was that I could speak in an American accent." This realization made her aware of the subtle dynamics of leadership selection early on in her life. As she continued, she noted, "The reason they weren't chosen was not that I was better than them but because I was more palatable."

That experience made Anila quickly realize the responsibility of being a leader who advocates for and brings diverse perspectives and stories to the table. It's why she has spent her entire career as a diversity, equity, and inclusion practitioner despite the challenges she has faced with her career choice. Immigrants are almost always expected to be scientists or engineers. She has had to constantly prove herself and has experienced the exhaustion of having to perform and conform to certain expectations. She has endured frustrating feelings of being tokenized by the superficial aspects of diversity, such as simply being a person of color or a woman. She witnessed firsthand the biases surrounding accents and appearances, which affect the perception of intelligence and leadership capabilities.

Addressing unconscious bias as it relates to immigrants involves recognizing them first.

ACCENT BIAS

English. Whose language is it, anyway?

I had a colleague who repeatedly attempted to complete, correct, and finish the sentences of an immigrant teammate.

> "Let's schedule a meeting to discuss the project timeline and create a timetable for each task."

> Colleague: "Ah, we usually call it a schedule in the US, and we often use the term agenda for what we plan to cover in a meeting."

> "I will meet you at the lift after the meeting, and we can head out to lunch."

Colleague: "Here in the US, we generally say elevator instead of lift, but yes, I'll meet you at the elevator."

I cringed.

English is the global language of business, spoken by over 1.5 billion people, with around 75 percent being nonnative English speakers.[1] Despite this, biases against nonnative English speakers persist in the workplace, impacting their perceived success, intelligence, and credibility.

Accent bias is a common challenge faced by nonnative English speakers. For every brilliant and talented nonnative English-speaking immigrant I have ever met, the ability for them to pursue other professional or educational goals in America went beyond their mastery of English. It almost always hinged on something else—their ability to communicate, as Anila puts it, in a "palatable way" to the dominant culture.

Diversity and inclusion efforts often focus on race, ethnicity, age, and gender, but language-related biases are equally important to address. Research indicates that nonnative English speakers are sometimes not given due credit, and unconscious bias against them is prevalent.[2] A study by Mayflower College in Plymouth, England, suggests that nonnative English speakers rarely receive the credit they deserve, and there is considerable unconscious bias against them.[3] Their research of one thousand nonnative English speakers showed that 88 percent find it more challenging to communicate with a native English speaker than with another nonnative speaker because native speakers typically do not know how to adjust their English for their audience.

Accent bias in the workplace, where communication nuances impact perceptions of intelligence and success, exacerbates the challenges nonnative English speakers face. Native English speakers may struggle to understand these challenges, especially if they haven't experienced the complexities of learning a foreign language.

Education systems in English-speaking countries often emphasize sophisticated language use, rewarding mastery of the language. However, effective communication with international English speakers may require a different approach, emphasizing tolerance and understanding rather than linguistic mastery.

Associating certain accents with intelligence or sophistication is an implicit bias deeply ingrained in societal perceptions. For instance, the belief that the British accent sounds smart transcends factors like race, class, and nationalism, shaping early impressions.

Questions about accents, such as "Where is the accent from?" are common for nonnative English speakers. I get asked that often in the workplace, at networking receptions, and even standing in the grocery store checkout line. I was once dumbfounded and left in an awkward moment of silence when asked this question. But over time, I have built a repertoire of polite retorts that I give with a smile.

As a lawyer, I write a lot. I often communicate with clients and opposing counsel over email long before I talk with them. I already have a peculiar name that carries with it a presumption that I am foreign. For this reason, I usually get the esteemed praise that I am "articulate" for being an immigrant.

So when I once connected with an opposing counsel for the first time, their comment, "I did not expect you to sound like that based on email exchanges," caused me great pause.

Being generally witty, I am rarely at a loss for words. However, we stood there, holding a long awkward silence, before I finally mustered the response, "What did you expect me to sound like?"

The fact of the matter is that most of us don't control how we speak the English language. It is a function of upbringing. It is a function of the age at which we learned the language, especially the accent from whom it is learned.

In her bestselling book *English with an Accent: Language, Ideology, and Discrimination in the United States*, Professor Rosina Lippi-Green scrutinizes American attitudes toward language.[4] Drawing from examples in various contexts—the classroom, the court, the media, and corporate culture—she exposes how discrimination based on accent supports and perpetuates social structures and unequal power relations. She argues that linguistic discrimination is a form of prejudice that can have serious consequences for individuals.

Leadership representation further perpetuates and reflects accent bias. Think about it for a second. When was the last time you had a senior leader with an accent? In my twenty years of work experience, I have only had *two*, and they came almost fifteen years into my career. With accents noticeably absent in senior leadership roles, addressing accent bias requires raising awareness, promoting inclusive communication, and challenging linguistic proficiency and intelligence assumptions. Creating a workplace that values diverse linguistic backgrounds contributes to a more inclusive and equitable environment.

The argument here is clear. English should be a tool for communication, not a measure of intelligence and certainly not a measure of leadership. Language acquisition is a facet of education, not education itself. One can read, write, and speak in their native language and still embody education and intelligence. UNESCO research supports the idea that starting education in one's mother tongue provides a stronger foundation.[5] Why, then, have accents become synonymous with one's intellectual capabilities?

One of Professor Lippi-Green's analyses focused on over three hundred characters from twenty-four Disney films spanning from 1938 to 1994, which is illuminating. Lippi-Green found that 40 percent of characters portrayed as evil or bad were nonnative English speakers with accents.[6] Disney films, often exploring themes of good versus evil, heavily rely on language and accents to shape characters quickly, perpetuating distorted views of people from different races or national origins, whether intentionally or unintentionally.

A friend of mine shared a disturbing incident that illustrates this issue. She called me upset. She had been part of the recruitment team for a new leader. She was tasked with narrowing down résumés to the top three for interviews. Naturally, she pared down the list of candidates based on qualifications and passed them on. When she checked in with the person who was conducting interviews to see how they went, they said they had chosen not to interview one individual because their accent was so thick when they called to schedule interviews. They feared the person would not be "a fit" because no one else would understand them despite their qualifications for the job. The candidate was an immigrant.

Recognizing this, corporations are responsible for eradicating accent bias in the workplace. According to professor of linguistics Tej K. Bhatia, accent discrimination "is the most powerful and overlooked feature responsible for social discrimination."[7] Talent development professionals and leaders should integrate an effective language management strategy into their diversity and inclusion plans beyond merely raising awareness of unconscious bias against international English speakers. The strategy should also guide native speakers in adjusting their communication styles with immigrant colleagues and customers.

The impact of accent bias can vary depending on several factors, such as the immigrants' location, industry, and individual experiences. However, it is undeniable that the impact of accent bias can be significant, with many immigrants reporting adverse effects on their self-esteem, career prospects, and overall well-being.

International leadership expert Carolina Donis offers an alternative viewpoint, advocating for celebrating accents as integral part of leadership, asserting, "Leadership is visual." She emphasizes that immigrants should be encouraged to embrace their differences, beginning with owning their accents, speaking confidently, and using their unique voices to engage others while dismantling stereotypes along the way.

Carolina, born and raised in Guatemala, is the cofounder of the Guatemala Próspera Foundation, which is aimed at nurturing leaders in her home country. Carolina's leadership journey took a fortunate turn when she met and partnered with John Maxwell to establish the country's transformation initiative, a program designed to develop leaders globally. For her, the experience highlighted the visual nature of leadership and why it is necessary for people to see examples they can relate to.

I see it yet another way: listening to someone with an accent compels us to listen more attentively. Effective communication transcends flawless pronunciation. It's about articulating ideas and forging connections. By fostering an environment where immigrants can confidently express their thoughts, you break down biases and unveil their leadership potential.

To further dismantle accent bias in the workplace, consider these strategies:

> **AWARENESS AND EDUCATION:** Organizations should provide awareness and education on accent bias. This could include training sessions, workshops, or seminars highlighting the benefits of having a diverse workforce and the negative impact of accent bias.
>
> **CREATE A CULTURE OF INCLUSION:** Organizations should foster a culture of inclusion where all employees feel valued and respected, regardless of their accent. This could include creating an open-door policy, encouraging open communication, and elevating leaders with accents to give company-wide presentations.

STANDARDIZED COMMUNICATION: Organizations could adopt a standardized communication style to reduce accent bias. This could include using simple language, avoiding jargon, and slowing the pace of speech. Additionally, the recruitment process should ensure that accent bias is not a factor in the selection process. This could include training recruiters on identifying and avoiding accent bias and reviewing job descriptions to ensure they do not have unnecessary language requirements.

FOREIGN EDUCATION BIAS

Researchers have long observed that foreign-educated immigrants earn lower wages and hold less-skilled jobs than US natives with the same educational attainment level. Still, the reasons for the disparity have been less clear. This issue will grow more salient as the average education level of immigrants rises. According to the Annual Social and Economic Supplement of the Current Population Survey, the share of recent working-age immigrants with at least a bachelor's degree rose from 34 percent in 2007 to 49 percent by 2021.[8]

Foreign education bias occurs when employers undervalue or misunderstand qualifications from educational institutions outside their country. There are two million college-educated, work-authorized immigrants and refugees in the US with expertise in critical industries, but systemic barriers stemming from foreign education bias prevent them from being able to put their experience and expertise to work in the US. This is a waste of human capital and potential.

Getting a professional license is an immediate and challenging hurdle for professionals in highly regulated industries like health care. Many licensing processes do not recognize experience or credentials earned abroad. Therefore, the pathway to rebuilding one's career requires repeating years of education and training. The result is an expensive and time-consuming process that keeps many out of their professional fields.

The barriers within other industries are just as challenging. Employers must recognize the value of degrees from unfamiliar universities or work experience in unknown companies. Newcomers also need more professional networks in the US. Most Americans get their jobs through someone they know, so it is difficult for newcomers to break through.

What I can say for certain is that the law of gravity remains identical irrespective of where and how people learn it, be it at a university in Nigeria, Turkey, or Taiwan or taught in English, Arabic, or Swahili.

The lack of recognition of education content being similar, regardless of where it is learned, has resulted in biased certification programs that limit the career growth of competent immigrants in the US. This creates barriers to career advancement among skilled immigrants in the US, which affects 25 percent of highly skilled immigrants with foreign degrees. According to a 2022 study by BYU, they are experiencing what is known as skill underutilization, compared to 18 percent of US-born highly skilled employees.[9]

Consider the Engineer-in-Training (EIT) certification as an example. To attain this designation, one must pass the Fundamentals of Engineering (FE) exam, the initial step toward becoming a licensed professional engineer (PE) in the US. The requirements include graduating from an Accreditation Board for Engineering and Technology (ABET) accredited school. The ABET-accredited schools are all four-year university engineering programs and are mostly US-based schools. This ninety-year-old accreditation process, primarily for US-based engineering programs, only recognized the universal nature of engineering concepts in October 2020 when it began accrediting international universities.

Because I am an engineer, my example here naturally focuses on engineering, but this holds true for various fields such as biology (all human hearts are the same) and chemistry (the periodic table is consistent). Ultimately, the only requirement that truly matters should be passing the exam. Evaluating technical capabilities should hinge on successful exam performance rather than on where immigrants acquired these capabilities.

To further dismantle foreign education bias in the workplace, consider these strategies:

COLLABORATE WITH CREDENTIAL EVALUATION AGENCIES: Work closely with credential evaluation agencies to establish clear criteria for evaluating foreign qualifications. Ensure that the requirements align with the skills and competencies for the specific job roles within your company to establish consistent standards for evaluating foreign credentials. This consistency helps in maintaining fairness and transparency in the hiring process.

INCORPORATE CREDENTIAL EVALUATION IN THE RECRUITMENT PROCESS: Integrate the credential evaluation process into your recruitment procedures. This could involve requesting candidates to send their information to one of the company's selected credential evaluation agencies and then submitting credential evaluation reports alongside their original documents during the application process.

OFFER TRAINING TO HUMAN RESOURCES AND HIRING MANAGERS: Train HR professionals and hiring managers on understanding and interpreting credential evaluation reports. This will enable them to make informed decisions based on the evaluated qualifications.

Companies can actively address and eliminate foreign education bias by taking these steps to foster a more inclusive and diverse workplace. This collaboration with credential evaluation agencies contributes to creating a fair and equitable hiring process for candidates with qualifications from diverse educational backgrounds.

This is not an exhaustive list of the biases immigrants face— just the prevailing two. I can think of name bias as another one near the top. Rather than going through them all, confronting and eliminating those biases is more important.

CONFRONTING IMMIGRANT BIASES

Immigrants have long been perceived as a threat to the labor market, dating back to the origin of the Chinese Exclusion Act discussed in chapter 2. That prevailing bias is rooted in fears of competition for jobs. Despite these concerns, research consistently highlights the positive contributions of immigrants to economies and cultural diversity, bringing with them innovation and entrepreneurship.

Confirmation bias plays a role in perpetuating negative perceptions of immigrants. This is the practice in which individuals seek information that aligns with their existing stereotypes while ignoring evidence that challenges these biases. Addressing confirmation bias requires raising awareness and understanding how biases operate.

Awareness campaigns that educate individuals about the concept of bias and its impact on decision-making help to combat the unconscious bias impacting immigrants. This knowledge enables people to recognize and interpret their biases.

Alarmingly, only 19 percent of companies require bias training for employees involved in hiring, and a mere 4 percent require training for employees involved in performance reviews.[10] To be effective, bias training must teach employees to counteract immigrant biases in specific scenarios. If this type of training only teaches employees that bias exists without giving them the tools to take action, it will be ineffective or counterproductive.

Understanding the immigration process undertaken by immigrants is also necessary for disrupting bias. Deeper insight into the immigration process provides employees with an understanding of the challenges, sacrifices, and unique experiences their immigrant colleagues face. This knowledge cultivates empathy, creating a supportive and inclusive environment where everyone feels valued and respected. Employees who comprehend the immigration process develop stronger camaraderie and support for their immigrant colleagues. Such understanding showcases an organization's commitment to addressing the unconscious biases unique to immigrants.

CHAPTER 6

ABSENCE OF IMMIGRANT LEADERSHIP

Why aren't there more immigrant CEOs?

This question consumed my thoughts for months, long before I began to write this book. It became the driving force behind my exploration into the dynamics of corporate leadership. It ignited a passionate inquiry into what factors dictate who ascends to the upper echelons of power within corporations. I found myself examining the subtle yet pervasive influences that shape organizational hierarchies. It became evident that the absence of immigrant CEOs was not merely a matter of chance but a reflection of broader structural inequalities and entrenched biases within corporate ecosystems.

While minority populations, in general, are underrepresented in leadership positions, the lack of immigrants is particularly noteworthy. Immigrants are 14 percent of the US population,[1] yet only 3 percent of Fortune 100 CEOs.[2] That math does not add up. Zooming out to look at Fortune 500 companies, there are fifty-six immigrant CEOs, with only four being immigrant women. This alarming statistic gains weight when considering that approximately twenty-one million female immigrants live in the US. It's a dismal reality, demanding urgent attention and action to rectify the persistent gaps of immigrants in corporate leadership.

A 2017 study by Sami Mahroum and Rashid Ansari titled "What the Data Tells Us About Immigrant Executives in the US" stands out as one of the few attempts to explore the presence of immigrants in leadership roles.[3] The authors conclude that to get the best leaders, the US needs to "embrace immigration and acknowledge the significant contribution that immigrant executives already play." One significant contribution is that they enrich decision-making at the leadership level.

Although practitioner magazines and industry journals often feature anecdotal stories of successful immigrant leaders, there is a noticeable scarcity of systematic academic research examining the reasons behind the glaring absence of immigrant leadership. This gap raises essential questions about the effectiveness of leadership development and who the impact of diversity, equity, and inclusion efforts benefits. Immigrants are projected to make up one in five of the US workforce by 2035. Leadership needs to start reflecting the future workforce.

You might be wondering why the absence of immigrant leadership matters.

In the fall of 2023, I had the honor of delivering the keynote address at the annual Women in Intellectual Property (IP) Law breakfast. The room, filled with approximately three hundred attendees, were predominantly women in the IP legal field. Also in the room were law students aspiring to carve a path in the field. Following my speech was a networking session for professionals of color to connect and share insights. During this gathering I found myself engaged in a conversation with a group of recent graduates, eager to navigate their journey of personal and professional growth.

True to my nature, I seized the moment to extend a hand in mentorship. I recognized the importance of imparting wisdom and guidance to the next generation, knowing firsthand the profound impact such guidance can have on one's professional trajectory. I offered them the opportunity to connect virtually.

A young woman, who I will call Ann for the sake of anonymity, instantly took me up on the offer. During my virtual meeting with Ann—who identifies as an Indian woman and who came to the US to pursue a law degree— she told me what would *really* help her career.

"I wish we could have more multicultural leaders such as you, who truly understand our versatile and different lived experiences... I could really use a boss I look up to, who can relate to me and what I've gone through as an immigrant," she said.

It's true, as American lawyer, educator, and civil rights activist Marian Wright Edelman said, "You can't be what you can't see."[4] We rely on stories, examples, leaders, and images to shape our understanding of who we are and our potential. Without these, we remain unaware and unable to become that which we cannot see.

THE FIRST IMMIGRANT CEO

In the summer of 2006, just two years after graduating from the University of Maine, I read a *New York Times* article with the headline "A Woman to Be Chief at PepsiCo" that captured my attention.[5] I was in the midst of completing my application to begin an MBA program at the University of Massachusetts Lowell. Hyperaware of the scarcity of female CEOs at the time, the woman featured in the story intrigued me for much more than her gender. She was the first immigrant to lead a Fortune 50 company.[6] That woman, Indra Nooyi, is one of the world's most admired business leaders. *Forbes* listed her in its World's 100 Most Powerful Women every year between 2007 and 2014, and Fortune named her number one on its annual ranking of Most Powerful Women in Business from 2006 to 2010.[7]

Nooyi, born in India, grew up in a close-knit family with two siblings, her parents, and her grandparents. She earned both her bachelor's degree and MBA from well-respected universities in India, commencing her career there at a textile firm and later as a product manager for Johnson & Johnson. In 1978, Nooyi came to the United States on a scholarship to attend Yale University, graduating with a master's degree in public and private management.

She then joined Boston Consulting Group (BCG) as a strategy consultant. From 1986 to 1994, she worked at Motorola and ABB, leading corporate strategy and planning departments. Nooyi joined PepsiCo in 1994, ascending through the ranks and serving in various leadership roles before becoming chief financial officer (CFO) and president in 2001. She joined the board of directors that same year. Five years later, she was named chairman and chief executive officer (CEO). Nooyi served as the CEO of PepsiCo from 2006 to 2018.[8]

When Raju Narisetti of McKinsey Global Publishing interviewed Nooyi about her memoir, *My Life In Full*, Nooyi discussed how her immigrant experience significantly shaped her leadership at PepsiCo.[9] She highlighted the advantage she gained in understanding the importance of respecting different cultures and perspectives when deciding to enter new markets. During the interview, she shared her enduring sense of being an immigrant in various settings, expressing that she'd walk into a room and think, "I'm so different; nobody else here looks like me... I just had that complex."[10]

To overcome that complex, Nooyi grounded herself in what she knew—her technical expertise, stating, "I focused on the knowledge base, on competence, on thinking about the issue at the detail level and a higher level."[11] She earned people's ears, trust, and respect, and soon enough, she was invited to most meetings, even when the discussion wasn't directly related to her area of work. Interestingly, they sought her point of view.

Her confidence to use hard work and deep knowledge to gain respect and trust came from a positive experience as an international student at Yale. She didn't know what to wear for her first summer job interview. Her clothes were either Indian clothing or jeans and tops. She saw most people wore suits for an interview, so she bought herself one, which cost less than fifty dollars because it was all she could afford. "It looked pretty bad. And people laughed at me when I walked into the career office,"[12] Nooyi recalls in jest. "But it was too late because I had an interview and needed the job."[13]

For her following interview, taking the advice of a career office staff who emphasized being true to herself, Nooyi wore a sari, a traditional staple of Indian clothing. She felt more comfortable in the sari. Ironically, she got both jobs. But that early experience taught her a crucial lesson and allowed Nooyi to infuse her Indian heritage into the workplace comfortably.

Nooyi also successfully formed relationships based on trust and respect earned through her work ethic. She understood that cultural integration went beyond adopting language and customs; it involved fostering genuine connections and understanding colleagues' perspectives. She actively sought opportunities to collaborate and engage with people from diverse backgrounds and valued their insights and experiences. On one occasion, she invited her boss over for traditional Indian chai at her house—a gesture to strengthen their relationship and expose her boss to her culture.

The other side of her success—that is, the side of success not attributed to anything she did— Nooyi attributes to supportive leaders. "They would say, 'What does Indra have to say on this topic?'"[14] she recalls. By explicitly stating this, they were signaling to others Nooyi's value: "They were giving me an indirect boost."[15]

This combination of her hard work and the boost from leaders, ensuring she was at the decision-making table with other senior executives, ultimately landed Nooyi the CEO role.

THE OTHER SIDE

This book is about the other side.

Nooyi recognized in her leadership journey, "It's not just hard work." The other side elevates immigrants to leadership. Immigrants generally work pretty hard. Immigration policies make sure of it. But, as Nooyi's story illustrates, the unique perspectives drawn from the immigrant experience, sponsored by leaders who believe in them, elevates immigrants to leadership.

To unravel the other side, the unexplored facets of success is to unravel the subtle yet powerful forces that can propel immigrants to realize their full potential. It navigates the interplay between determination and the systems designed to capitalize on it. PepsiCo enhanced profitability and magnified Nooyi's influence by being an environment supportive of immigrants. This is evident through initiatives like PepsiCo's 2022 commitment to hiring five hundred refugees over three years in the United States.[16]

Immigration is often discussed in broad political and policy terms, focusing on its effects on labor markets, schools, and social services. However, at its core, immigration profoundly influences individuals and their identities in deeply personal ways. Immigrants make the bold choice to leave their home countries and communities, facing unfamiliar terrain, language barriers, and cultural nuances with courage and determination. It's not just about relocating; it's about reimagining life, which requires adaptability, learning, and relearning.

For many, the pursuit of the American Dream is the driving force behind why they embark on the immigrant journey. But it's not solely about material success; it's about the promise of opportunity, the chance to rewrite one's destiny, and the belief that hard work can open doors. We often focus on the beauty of the American Dream without fully evaluating what it means to achieve and maintain it, especially today. It's time to go beyond the fairytale and acknowledge the contributions that immigrants make in pursuit of those dreams are leadership competencies.

An immigrant rising to be CEO of a Fortune 500 company is rare and remarkable, yet it is also supposed to be how America works—oversimplified, perhaps, yet emblematic of the American Dream. Shockingly, despite the potential and qualifications of immigrants, many employers remain hesitant to consider immigrants for senior leadership roles. A survey conducted by the Peel Halton Workforce Development Group of 484 Canadian organizations revealed that 37 percent of organizations would not even entertain the idea of hiring immigrants for such positions.[17]

Such reluctance is confounding, particularly when considering the invaluable contributions of immigrants to the robust start-up economy in both the Canadian and American start-up economy. Indeed, immigrants have been the driving force behind more than half (55 percent) of America's start-up companies valued at $1 billion or more, as elucidated by the National Foundation for American Policy research.[18] These immigrant-founded companies boast an aggregate value surpassing $1.2 trillion, exceeding the combined value of companies listed on the primary stock markets of several nations.[19]

Moreover, the impact of these immigrant-founded companies extends far beyond mere valuation, with each entity generating an average of 859 jobs.[20] So if immigrants can successfully create unicorn companies, why are they not entrusted with leadership roles in publicly traded corporations? According to Pamela Jeffery, founder of the Canadian Board Diversity Council, the answer lies in pervasive biases that undermine the perceived expertise of immigrants, echoing the challenges that other marginalized groups like women face in leadership roles.[21] This troubling reality needs to be addressed and dismantle.

In the book titled *The Hard Thing about Hard Things*, Ben Horowitz of leading venture capital firm Andreessen Horowitz emphasizes that a key challenge for CEOs is balancing strategic vision with operational execution.[22] He believes founding CEOs often excel at vision but may need help as their companies grow more complex.[23] However, executing amid uncertainty and change is paramount in today's business landscape. We need CEOs who can articulate a compelling vision while inspiring and empowering their teams to execute through uncertainty.

THE GLOBAL ECONOMY

Every company is grappling with some form of disruption. At every turn lies uncertainty. The immigrant experience breeds an acceptance of forces beyond our control as well as the need to persevere despite them. This allows innovation and patience with processes to coexist in a corporate bureaucracy. A leader must be able to adapt to what's shaping our marketplace.

One of the key strengths of immigrant leadership lies in its ability to bridge cultural divides and forge connections across borders. Immigrant leaders possess a deep understanding of different cultures, languages, and business practices, enabling them to navigate international markets with agility and adaptability. This cultural fluency allows immigrant leaders to build strong relationships with stakeholders from diverse backgrounds, fostering collaboration and driving business growth on a global scale.

Moreover, immigrant leaders often bring a fresh perspective to traditional business practices, challenging conventional wisdom and driving innovation. Their experiences of adapting to new environments and overcoming obstacles instill a spirit of resilience and creativity, which can inspire transformative change within organizations.

The prevailing narrative suggests that in America, anyone with enough grit and determination can ascend the ranks of corporate power, regardless of their background or origins. However, this idealized notion belies the harsh realities faced by immigrants navigating corporate America. The journey from immigrant to CEO is fraught with obstacles—from cultural barriers and implicit biases to systemic inequities ingrained within the very fabric of our society.

As we peel back the layers of this narrative, we are confronted with a sobering truth. The path to CEO for immigrants is often strewn with challenges and setbacks that extend far beyond personal ambition and tenacity. Sometimes, structural and process issues are in place, so it's not all bias-driven. Some of it is process-driven, which we will explore fully throughout part 3 of this book.

Only when we start peeling back the layers and looking deeper at what's happening can we start to understand why it's happening. Our collective responsibility is to dismantle the barriers that obstruct the path because it's costing us our competitive advantage in the global economy. Managers and leaders with a global perspective are essential if companies want to succeed in the global marketplace. And what better way to get that perspective than from leaders who have foreign, intersectional, or multicultural backgrounds?

CHAPTER 7

INFLUENCE OF IMMIGRANT LEADERSHIP

The topic of leadership echoes through academic corridors, HR offices, and boardrooms alike. A staggering number of leadership books are written each year, and companies spend billions on leadership development. The quest for defining good leadership is marked by debates on whether leaders are born or made. However, within these debates, one truth stands. Anyone can cultivate the characteristics and skills needed to be a leader.

Research consistently indicates that organizations with top-notch leaders are thirteen times more likely to outperform their competitors across key metrics like financial performance, product and service quality, employee engagement, and customer satisfaction. Leaders must possess exceptional talent as well as the ability to attract followers to lead effectively. At its core, leadership is the art of influencing others to take action. Simple, right? Yet a Google search for "how to be a good leader" yields over 115 million results.

I like the simplicity of what my ten-year-old daughter considers as a leader: "someone who inspires and helps others to be better." That's right, baby girl, many can differ on what leadership is or what it means, but ultimately, we can all agree that a leader is someone who can effectively guide, inspire, and motivate others toward a common goal while also fostering a culture of trust, respect, and collaboration.

Immigrant leadership is a strategic asset for corporations navigating the complexities of the modern business environment. It fosters innovation, improves decision-making, enhances global market understanding, attracts top talent, positively impacts financial performance, and contributes to a solid and reputable brand.

THE INFLUENCE OF IMMIGRANT LEADERSHIP ON PROFITABILITY

Leadership directly influences a company's financial performance. Research consistently demonstrates that strong leadership correlates with increased profitability through various mechanisms. PepsiCo—currently the second-largest food and beverage company globally, boasting approximately $63 billion in revenues—owes much of this achievement to Nooyi. Under her guidance, the company increased its profitability, an impressive feat under any circumstances but especially during the 2008 financial crisis.[1] Nooyi transformed PepsiCo, consistently steering the company in a profit-making direction while improving environmental sustainability, introducing healthier offerings, and making the company community-centered.

Throughout her remarkable career at PepsiCo, Nooyi navigated challenges such as shifting consumer tastes, rising health concerns, economic hardship, and increasing competition in the beverage and snack industry. Known for her innovative thinking and strategic approaches, she drove growth and profitability for the company through bold initiatives and strategic moves, including the acquisition of Quaker Oats and Tropicana as well as the development of new products and brands such as Gatorade and Naked Juice.[2]

Her visionary leadership inspired and motivated employees to achieve higher levels of performance. Leaders who articulate a clear vision and goals for the organization foster a sense of purpose among employees, driving them to work toward common objectives. For example, a study published in the *Journal of Business Studies* found that companies led by visionary leaders experienced higher levels of financial performance due to improved employee engagement and commitment.[3] This, in turn, reduces turnover costs and enhances productivity, ultimately contributing to improved profitability.

THE INFLUENCE OF IMMIGRANT LEADERSHIP ON INNOVATION
Leadership also plays a pivotal role in fostering innovation, which maintains competitiveness in dynamic markets. Leaders who encourage creativity and experimentation empower their teams to explore new ideas and approaches, paving the way for the development of innovative products or services that can drive revenue growth.

Under Nooyi's leadership, one of the most innovative initiatives was redirecting Pepsi's considerable corporate spending away from junk foods and into healthier alternatives. Dietary balance was a key feature of Nooyi's strategy from day one. At a time when many food companies were researching and developing new flavors, Pepsi was creating recipes that were lower in salt and fat.

Nooyi recognized at a pretty early stage that consumer trends were changing. To carry out the plan that became her legacy, she made big hires that tipped her commitment to healthier eating. She hired Pepsi's first chief scientific officer, Mehmood Khan, and its first director of global health policy, Derek Yach.[4] Two thoughtful immigrant hires, if I may add. Then she reclassified Pepsi's wide-ranging products into three categories, designed to give customers more information about the foods they consume: "fun for you" (such as potato chips and regular soda), "better for you" (diet or low-fat versions of snacks and fizzy drinks), and "good for you" (for example, the recently acquired Quaker Oats oatmeal).[5]

She then declared that Pepsi needed to be part of the solution to "one of the world's biggest public health challenges—a challenge fundamentally linked to our industry: obesity."[6] For example, Gatorade is now marketed specifically toward athletes, rather than being advertised as an everyday recreational beverage.

Research conducted by *Harvard Business Review* suggests that companies with innovative leaders like Nooyi who influence innovation outperform their competitors, demonstrating higher profitability over time.[7]

THE INFLUENCE OF LEADERSHIP ON ORGANIZATIONAL CULTURE

Everything a leader does shapes the organization's culture, and culture, in turn, influences organizational success.

Culture, defined as the collective set of beliefs and attitudes about how things are done in a workplace, is a sum of formal and informal systems, behaviors, and values. This intangible force is felt universally in an organization, influencing every aspect of work. The impact of company culture extends far beyond mere abstraction, significantly shaping vital metrics to organizational success. From financial performance and employee retention to enhancing innovation and customer service, the reverberations of a well-cultivated culture are profound. A skilled leader understands their pivotal role in cultivating and steering this cultural force, recognizing that it reflects the organization's identity and is a driving force behind its achievements.

Nooyi recognized the influence her leadership had on culture and understood that cultural integration was a continuous process, requiring a genuine commitment to personal growth and development. She actively sought feedback and embraced diverse perspectives, allowing her to adapt her leadership style to meet the evolving needs of the organization. One such occasion was when the company was getting ready to enter a new market. She requested a local consultant to spend time educating her on the nuances of the culture in that new market. She instinctively knew as an immigrant who had worked in the business world in both India and in the US that effectively conducting business in a new country required cultural intelligence.

In addition to her internal efforts, Nooyi also recognized the importance of external partnerships and engagement with stakeholders across different cultures. She prioritized building strong relationships with international partners and stakeholders, understanding that global success required an understanding of local markets and consumer preferences. Nooyi was also known for her strong commitment to sustainability and corporate responsibility and led efforts to reduce PepsiCo's environmental footprint while promoting healthier products.

Nooyi's leadership is an inspiring example of immigrant leadership. Her story highlights the broader narrative of how immigrant leadership boosts business growth, supercharges company culture, and propels innovation.

* * *

Building leadership capability has become one of the highest priorities on the business agenda.

There has been a shift in leadership requirements for the twenty-first century. Themes such as inclusivity, social responsibility, digital proficiency, and adept navigation of network dynamics are now integral to leadership principles. Business success is measured beyond financial metrics in the current social enterprise era. Scrutiny extends to its impact on the social and physical environment, customer relationships, and interactions with employees and collaborators. Leaders fixated solely on operational efficiency and market competition are short-sighted and need a comprehensive engagement with the broader challenges of the business.

Alice Eagly and Jean Lau Chin, prominent American clinical psychologists recognized for their work on diversity in leadership and cultural competence, have highlighted the infrequent consideration of the influence of cultural diversity on leadership.[8] They argue that this oversight weakens our ability to tackle contemporary leadership challenges effectively. These challenges include limited access of individuals from diverse identity groups to leadership roles, the influence of leaders' dual identities, and the potential for excellent leadership from groups traditionally excluded from such roles due to their differences from conventional leaders.

While practitioner magazines and industry journals often feature anecdotal stories of successful immigrant leaders, there is a noticeable scarcity of systematic academic research examining how members of immigrant and minority groups attain leadership roles. This gap raises essential questions about leadership development theory, the lessons that can be derived from immigrant experiences in accessing leadership positions, and how leaders from diverse identity groups lead.

THE MISALIGNMENT BETWEEN LEADERSHIP REQUIREMENTS AND EXISTING TALENT

For most organizations, leadership development lags behind the pace of change, fueling a lack of confidence in the current leadership's ability to steer transformative paths for the future. Immigrants bring bold and visionary perspectives to the business world. Although immigrants significantly contribute to organizational dynamics, organizations pay less attention to their leadership potential.

Addressing this issue requires action. As Atefeh Riazi, CIO of the Hearst Media Group and former CIO of the United Nations, emphasizes in an interview, it is important to dismantle the barriers that block immigrants' unique capabilities, motivations, and opportunities for leadership performance.[9] These barriers include language proficiency barriers, cross-cultural competency, and adjustment barriers, intergroup bias barriers due to immigrant status, and strategic integration barriers. We'll talk about all these in depth in the chapters ahead.

Workplaces must actively dismantle these obstacles to unlock the full potential of immigrant leaders. Beyond individual benefits, this approach contributes to creating more inclusive workplaces, nurturing more leaders, fixing the gaps in leadership pipelines, and ultimately improving operational success.

THE INFLUENCE OF DIVERSE LEADERSHIP IN CORPORATIONS

In today's business environment where diversity, equity, and inclusion (DEI) efforts are increasingly important, where more individuals from underrepresented groups are being hired, and where understanding diversity is essential, a boss with an intersectional foreign background is ideal. Leaders like this can understand and relate to a multitude of different lived experiences and can more easily manage a team of diverse individuals.

A *Harvard Business Review* article states that developing a diverse leadership pipeline offers significant advantages across all sectors.[10] And a well cited study by McKinsey & Company found firms with ethnically diverse executive teams were 33 percent more likely to outperform their peers on profitability.[11] Similarly, those with gender diversity at the executive level had a 21 percent likelihood of outperforming industry competitors.[12]

Now, leaders are expected to possess cultural competence and navigate effectively across different cultures in a world of global interconnectedness and a rapidly diversifying workforce. Additionally, there is an increasing expectation for leadership representation from various identity groups. Without diverse leadership, organizations will struggle not just operationally but in creating a vibrant company culture that engages the workforce and attracts top talent.

Diverse leadership is no longer a mere buzzword. It's a strategic imperative for corporations aiming to excel in the complex and dynamic global landscape. Its importance goes beyond social responsibility. It's intricately linked to profitability, enhanced innovation, improved decision-making, and overall business success.

On diverse leadership teams, individuals bring a range of backgrounds, experiences, and perspectives, fostering innovation and creativity in problem-solving and product development. This diversity of thought results in more robust decision-making processes, challenging assumptions, and considering a broader range of potential outcomes.

Understanding diverse markets is critical in the global economy, and a leadership team mirroring the diversity of the workplace and customer base enhances this understanding. It allows for better adaptation to varied cultural nuances, preferences, and trends, tailoring strategies to meet the needs of a diverse clientele. Commitment to diverse leadership becomes a powerful attractor for top talent. A workplace that celebrates unique skills and perspectives fosters employee satisfaction and retention, contributing to a positive organizational culture.

Studies consistently indicate a positive correlation between diverse leadership and improved financial performance.[13] Companies with diverse leadership demonstrate adaptability, address market changes, and showcase resilience, ultimately leading to sustained financial success. Avon Corporation provides a notable example. Initially facing low profitability in US inner city markets, the company improved results substantially by giving authority over these markets to Black and Hispanic managers. Consequently, these once-unprofitable sectors became the most productive of Avon's US markets.[14] Gannett News Media's experience also illustrates leveraging cultural leadership for improving market share. The early marketing success of *USA Today* was primarily attributable to the presence of people from various cultural backgrounds in daily news meetings.[15]

Beyond financial considerations, diverse leadership is integral to a corporation's brand reputation. Stakeholders and consumers increasingly support organizations prioritizing diversity and inclusion, viewing them as socially responsible and committed to positive values.

PART III

CHAPTER 8

UNDERSTANDING IMMIGRIT

Understand /verb/ to know the meaning of something

In her TED Talk "Grit: The Power of Passion and Perseverance," which has been viewed over thirteen million times, psychologist Angela Duckworth defines grit as "perseverance and passion for long-term goals."[1] Since her 2013 TED Talk, Duckworth's theory of grit has received much attention and discussion. Those who believe in the power of grit aren't always sure how to develop or encourage it.[2]

Grit is more than just working hard; it's about staying committed to a task or goal, even when faced with difficulties. Contrary to being an innate trait, individuals cultivate grit over time. It's a personality trait developed and nurtured through practice and experience. Because grit is developed, not bestowed, everyone possesses a varying amount. These levels of grit arise from our choices, actions, and responses to challenges.

Grit is a complex interplay of life experiences, mindset, passion, support systems, and the willingness to learn and adapt. Recognizing grit as a developed trait underscores the idea that everyone's journey is unique, and individuals have the agency to shape their resilience and perseverance over time.

Without question, *all* immigrants possess grit.

GRIT, PLUS SOME

Immigrants embody a dynamic and multifaceted form of grit. They embody ImmiGRIT, the amalgamation of grit, adaptability, resourcefulness, and resilience forged from their unique experiences. To face challenges like cultural adjustments, language barriers, building a new life, or navigating the immigration system, immigrants have to demonstrate remarkable perseverance.

Whether forcibly displaced or voluntarily chosen, immigrants pursue the dreams that led them to leave their home country. Doing so requires significant sacrifices and strenuous work. Their adaptability shines through as they navigate unfamiliar territories and embrace change. In the face of setbacks, immigrants persevere, learning from failures and pushing forward. That's ImmiGRIT. That's what makes immigrants exceptional leaders.

Let's delve into understanding the other components of ImmiGRIT.

ADAPTABILITY

"I had no choice but to adapt," Zainab, director at Procter & Gamble, reflects when describing her first day in America on the chilly January day she arrived in Grand Forks, North Dakota. January in North Dakota is cold for anyone, but especially for a sub-Saharan African accustomed to an average temperature of eighty-three degrees Fahrenheit.

Immigration and the ensuing intercultural experience demand adaptability. Consider that immigrants are compelled to adapt upon arriving in a new country. Immigration, whether voluntary or involuntary, involves a transition with numerous unknowns. What is known, however, is the sacrifice of social networks and familial bonds in exchange for survival. Being an immigrant means change. It implies disruptions to interpersonal systems and social networks and challenges to one's system of meaning. It means adapting to new idioms and contexts, involving the integration of identities and cultural systems.

Before Zainab became my roommate during my second semester at the University of Maine, she had spent a semester at the University of North Dakota. When we chose to become roommates, we had two things in common. We were both engineering students and international students from Nigeria. Beyond that, we grew up differently. Over the more than two decades of our friendship, we have come to appreciate how our now almost second-nature wizardry at adaptability developed from our immigrant experience.

Living in Nigeria, Zainab experienced the vibrancy of a metropolitan environment where anything was readily available. The transition from Lagos to North Dakota proved jarring in many ways, immediately challenging Zainab to adapt. There was the stark environmental shift from the bustling metropolis of Lagos to the small town of Grand Forks. There was also the transition from the equatorial climate of Lagos to the frigid winters of North Dakota, compounded by her arrival in the heart of winter.

It became necessary to quickly learn to navigate the extreme cold and make practical adjustments, such as utilizing tunnels to shield herself from the cold while commuting across campus. Beyond weather adjustments, Zainab faced cultural and social differences in North Dakota. The food, clothing, and overall lifestyle deviated dramatically from those in her Nigerian upbringing. Yet her unwavering focus on goals and laser-like determination to succeed helped her overcome those challenges. Zainab's primary objective was academic excellence and achieving her educational goals, giving her the drive and motivation to navigate the unfamiliar environment. In a recent conversation, she reflected, "I had to figure out a way to function and be good in school in that environment."

Zainab's story of her first days in America exemplifies adaptability—a shared trait among immigrants. In some form or fashion, immigrants adapt almost immediately. I faced a different challenge when I arrived in Orono, Maine, on a hot August day. When I arrived the night before campus housing opened, only one of my two suitcases was there. Late in the evening, with thoughts of a proper meal, a shower, and figuring out how to reach my parents in Nigeria, I settled into a hotel room with half my belongings. Move-in day was tough enough to handle alone, let alone with only half of my things.

"I'll figure it out," I told myself. I had no choice.

It is an oversimplification to define adaptability merely as a person's ability to adjust to changes. *Merriam-Webster Dictionary* defines adaptability as "adjusting to changes and becoming well-suited to new circumstances." Doing so takes practice. When immersed in a new culture, especially learning a new language, adaptability is not a one-time event but a continual daily requirement.

Adaptability is a skill acquired and honed only through practice, whether adapting to climate, food, spaces, or someone challenging your intelligence because of how you spell or sound when you speak. Adapting is a challenging and ongoing process that many would avoid if given the choice because it is uncomfortable. In an article, Helena Seo, head of design at DoorDash, shared her struggles with adapting as an immigrant from Korea, stating, "There were numerous times when I wanted to leave it all behind and go back to Korea where I could comfortably blend in... However, I didn't like the idea of resigning and was determined to stand on my feet in the US."[3] That's ImmiGRIT.

Over time, immigrants make modifications according to changing circumstances. Regardless of their background, immigrants tend to lose any sense of entitlement as they make those modifications to meet changing circumstances. This adaptability forces a reexamination of the familiar, demanding changes in thinking and action. Research by William Kerr, a Harvard Business School professor, highlights that the willingness to move globally, often leaving family behind, suggests a determination and tolerance for business risks. [4]

In today's dynamic world, adaptability is a highly regarded skill, ranking among the top five sought by employers. The ever-changing business landscape—influenced by market trends, mergers, acquisitions, and economic climates— requires a workforce capable of adapting swiftly. The COVID-19 pandemic has demonstrated the importance of flexibility, making adaptability a vital asset in any job.

Companies prioritizing adaptability can respond swiftly to changing customer needs, enhance decision-making processes, and accelerate innovation. Influential and respected leaders perceive change not as an obstacle but as an opportunity for growth or a window into possibilities. As discussed in the *Harvard Business Review* article "5 Principles to Guide Adaptive Leadership," adaptive leaders experiment, learn from failures, and make adjustments quickly, fostering a sense of purpose within their teams even amid change.[5]

Among the many attributes that mark a good leader, adaptability is paramount. How well a leader embraces shifts in the professional landscape and uses them to enhance the organization's trajectory can be a vital measure of effectiveness. Immigrants, uniquely skilled at employing adaptability, contribute to building this organizational muscle required for businesses to be more receptive and responsive to continual change.

Three ways immigrants enhance adaptability within teams and organizations:

1. **THEY CAN ADAPT TO RAPID TECHNOLOGICAL CHANGES:** In an era of unprecedented technological advancement, companies that swiftly adapt to new tools, platforms, and software are more likely to succeed. Immigrants comfortable with emerging technologies can facilitate the learning and adoption of new systems among their colleagues. Leveraging technology efficiently improves overall company performance.

2. **THEY BUILD AGILITY AND FLEXIBILITY:** The workforce is evolving in diversity, and companies

that can adapt to different working styles, skill sets, and generational differences are more likely to attract and retain top talent. Immigrants, with their flexibility and adaptability, contribute to making their companies more agile and responsive to evolving business needs. Their willingness to take on new roles or responsibilities enables quick pivots in response to market or industry changes.

3. **THEY PROMOTE DISRUPTIVE COMPETITION:** Disruptive start-ups are emerging in almost every industry, and companies that can quickly adapt to new market entrants and business models are more likely to survive. Immigrants contribute by being open to learning new skills, taking on new tasks, and seeking feedback to improve performance. Their approach fosters thinking outside the box and generates new ideas, positioning the company competitively in the market.

RESOURCEFULNESS

Imagine eagerly anticipating your sixteenth birthday, looking forward to visiting the Department of Motor Vehicles (DMV) for a driver's license, only to discover an unexpected barrier. Your immigration status renders you ineligible. This was the unforeseen predicament that Diego Corzo faced. Determined not to let this obstacle derail his ambitions, Corzo shared in his TEDxFSU talk an inspiring tale of the resourcefulness that immigrants showcase to overcome obstacles and flourish in the face of adversity.[6]

The dictionary defines resourcefulness as "the ability to find quick and clever ways to overcome difficulties." However, people often misunderstand resourcefulness. Some see it as coping with a lack while others perceive it as having abundant resources. Both miss the nuance of resourcefulness, which is about the *quick and clever* utilization of whatever resources are available.

Born in Lima, Peru, Corzo moved to the US with his family when he was nine. His life story as an immigrant navigating success in America was riddled with never-ending obstacles he faced and overcame with tenacity and resourcefulness. Corzo is one of the 11.7 million undocumented immigrants in the United States and one of the 800,000 Dreamers—what Congress calls a person who was brought into the country as a child and is currently undocumented.[7] Like many Dreamers, Diego discovered his undocumented status as a teenager when he could not get a driver's license or fill out financial aid forms for college due to the lack of a social security number. Yet Diego did not let this hinder his pursuit of the American Dream.

After graduating third in his high school class, Corzo was admitted to Florida State University. However, his undocumented status meant he didn't qualify for student loans or financial aid. Even scholarships won were rescinded. Determined, Corzo found a job at a nonprofit in the information technology (IT) department, only to discover that, due to his immigration status, he could not be hired.

During the TEDxFSU talk, Corzo told the audience, "I made a grim realization that not only can I not drive or get student loans, but now I can't get a job anywhere. But I didn't let that stop me." Digging deep, Corzo discovered he could apply for an employer identification number (EIN) and form a business despite lacking a social security number. That's right, an undocumented immigrant cannot be paid as an employee but can create businesses and pay business taxes. Uncle Sam always eats. (I digress.) Corzo started his own company as an IT independent contractor for various companies. His only mode of transportation was a bike, which was how he got around to his clients. Corzo's unwavering mindset was evident in the face of challenges, as he put it: "If the door of opportunity is closed, I go through the window."

The art of resourcefulness is learned through experiences and exposure to situations that demand strategic utilization of internal and external resources. It's about navigating situations to ensure current goals have a higher likelihood of success, both in the short and long term. Resourcefulness is about getting things done in the face of obstacles and constraints. This means approaching what's in front of you and optimizing what you have, whether solving a problem, making something new, or just thinking about how to do something better. Resourcefulness takes imagination and persistence while staying optimistic about the outcome. Resourcefulness also builds bonds.

When I arrived at my new dorm room on campus with that one suitcase, I had only half of what I would need. I had no bank account or phone—just the cash my parents had sent me off with. I knew no one. The cash on me did not anticipate needing to buy much beyond my books and emergency items till I could land a campus job. I had no idea how to get to the nearest store, and if I did, I was dealing with a different currency, so I had no idea how much things cost in comparison. As I started taking stock of what I had and would need with me, my new roommate arrived. She arrived with a whole convoy—her family.

Within two minutes, my new roommate and her family went from being strangers to becoming the only real source of information I had to secure the additional things I needed. In between trying to figure out how to get to a store and discussing how much I should anticipate a new set of underwear costing me while trying to convert currency in my head to see if the prices of things cost the same as in Nigeria, my roommate and I developed a level of relationship that would have been unlikely to grow in such a short time.

In leadership, resourcefulness is highly prized. When members of the Special Forces teams were asked the one trait they would want in a team leader, their answer was not superior physical ability, strategic intelligence, or command presence.[8] When it comes to the person whose leadership could mean the difference between life and death for the team, they prioritize resourcefulness or the ability to devise quick, creative ways to solve problems and overcome difficulties.

Resourcefulness and adaptability, innate in the immigrant experience, go hand-in-hand. The most resourceful leaders adapt to obstacles, gather information swiftly, shape environments, and build relationships purposefully to achieve tasks. Resourcefulness is also a mindset, consisting of a unique blend of optimism that things will work out and pragmatism to navigate challenges if they don't. In today's business environment, resourcefulness is not just about creating something entirely new but also about improving existing products. This trait is critical in good times and bad, fostering innovation and making old things work better.

At its essence, resourcefulness is about leading change, which is particularly critical when change catches us unaware and ill-prepared. In such circumstances, leaders embodying resourcefulness become even more essential.

Three ways immigrants emerge as resourceful leaders within teams and organizations:

1. **THEY ARE OPEN TO POSSIBILITIES:** Immigrant leaders encourage organizations to look beyond traditional approaches and focus on doing things differently for the sake of improvement. They foster an open culture where employees collaboratively work through solutions. Immigrants, having experienced alternative ways, collaborate effectively, showcasing a willingness to see things differently.

2. **THEY USE PERSONAL RESILIENCE AS A GUIDE:** Immigrant leaders draw strength from personal resilience, understanding that not every problem comes with a budget. Their tenacity and internal strength keep them open to new possibilities, navigating challenges with a mindset that transcends conventional solutions.

3. **THEY HAVE AN ABILITY TO SIMPLIFY:** Immigrant leaders possess a unique ability to simplify complex processes. They understand and have endured problematic procedures, enabling them to find more effective solutions. By getting into the details, they see the big picture, communicating their vision clearly to stakeholders and aligning everyone toward common goals.

TRANSFORMATIVE RESILIENCE

Rebecca Shi, executive director of the American Business Immigration Coalition (ABIC), recounts her mother's journey to achieve US citizenship in an essay, "The Resilience of Immigrants Is Rebuilding America."[9] Imagine enduring twenty-three years of waiting for citizenship, all the while grappling with the constant fear of deportation and the risk of losing everything you have painstakingly built. That's the unwavering resilience that immigrants embody.

Rebecca was ten when her parents immigrated to the US from China. Her father was a heart surgeon and her mother a pathologist. Her father came to the US for a postdoctoral program at Harvard School of Public Health. Then, a few years later, Rebecca and her mother joined him in Boston. Rebecca and her father got their green cards and later citizenship, but bad immigration legal advice resulted in her mother losing her legal status and effectively becoming an undocumented immigrant.

As an undocumented resident, immigration attorney after immigration attorney advised that Rebecca's mom "might get deported." Living constantly terrified of deportation, Rebecca's mom kept a low profile and worked for tips at Chinese restaurants. Those tips helped Rebecca get into the University of Chicago. The circumstances led Rebecca to join a movement of advocates trying to change the laws to protect her mother. Rebecca's advocacy worked; after twenty-three years of her mom living in the US, she became a citizen. At the age of sixty-three, Rebecca's mom returned to the medical profession, where she examines biopsy specimens to diagnose a range of illnesses like tumors and ulcers.[10]

Studies consistently show that immigrants exhibit higher resilience and psychological well-being levels than nonimmigrants.[11] This ability to maintain hope and optimism despite adversity is remarkable, considering the mental health risks associated with migration and resettlement in a new country.

But what is resilience? According to the American Psychological Association (APA), resilience is "the process of adapting well in the face of adversity, trauma, tragedy, threats, or significant sources of stress."[12] The definition of resilience has evolved over the years. Older research from 2009 describes it as the "development of competence despite severe or pervasive adversity." A recent study from 2018 acknowledges that resilience, especially concerning trauma and coping, is not easily defined and varies based on the individual.[13]

Regardless of the specific definition, the critical thing to remember is that resilience happens out of necessity. Resilience involves overcoming challenges while maintaining well-being and psychological stability in the face of stress or trauma. Importantly, resilience is not about avoiding or denying difficult experiences. Instead, it's about learning to manage these challenges in healthy ways that foster growth and well-being. It is not about enduring hardships to prove toughness, especially when alternatives exist. Resilience varies from person to person and is influenced by the capacity to navigate complex events, the severity of those events, and their impact on the individual.

Resilience can be measured by looking at a singular event. Many immigrants exhibit resilience in the singular event of entering a new country. Yet immigrants must navigate multiple challenges and adversities in relocating and adapting to a new country.[14] Immigrants often face a range of stressors, including many of which we have already discussed, such as cultural differences, language barriers, and loss of social support networks, all of which individually can be particularly challenging. Despite these difficulties, many immigrants can adapt and thrive in their new environment. That's resilience.

Once considered a secondary leadership trait, resilience has emerged as a top leadership skill. A survey by CEMS, a Global Alliance of business schools, multinational companies, and NGOs, found a significant shift in leadership perceptions.[15] The guide "Leadership in a Post-COVID-19 World" published by CEMS contains the survey results completed by over 1,700 cooperate leaders, revealing that before the pandemic, a mere 13 percent viewed resilience as an essential leadership trait, while post-pandemic this figure surged to 34 percent.[16]

Many of us are accustomed to colloquially referring to the term resilience as *bouncing back*, so when I came across the term transformative resilience while researching, I was immediately fascinated by this different construct of resilience as *springing forward*. This construct is explored in the award-winning book *Type R: Transformative Resilience for Thriving in a Turbulent World*.

Intrigued, I reached out to Ama Marston, coauthor of the book, to explore the concept of transformative resilience. In my insightful conversation with Ama, she explained transformative resilience as more nuanced than springing forward in that it is "the ability to learn, grow, and innovate from change, challenges, and disruption." Emphasis on learning and growing.

Marston also emphasized the six critical skills discussed in her book that are integral to transformative resilience: adaptability, continual learning, healthy control, leveraging support, a deep sense of purpose, and active engagement. With these skills, people evolve beyond the conventional experience of resilience, which typically involves bouncing back from adversity.[17] Instead, they develop the ability to spring forward from challenges and stressors, leveraging the experiences for personal growth, learning, and innovation.[18] This perspective aptly captures the nuanced and transformative nature of the immigrant experience. With adaptability when an immigrant encounters adversity, they evolve beyond the conventional experience of resilience.

My conversation with Marston captivated me for more than just her book and extensive research into transformative resilience. It only took me a short time into our dialogue to discern why. Her insights were deeply personal. Drawing from her journey as an immigrant in the UK, Marston observed how this firsthand experience significantly shaped her research and understanding of resilience and the unique challenges immigrants face. Marston candidly expressed, "Some of my most challenging years were spent as an immigrant in the UK." She shed light on the authenticity and depth of her insights.

A nonprofit organization initially brought Marston from America to the UK for work. Eventually outgrowing the sector, she started her own business. However, she encountered challenges with the immigration process, particularly the requirement to earn an additional £10,000 within a short timeframe to maintain her visa status. Talk about stress.

While navigating the complexities of starting a business, she also faced health setbacks and supported her father, who had been in a car accident and had undergone amputation in Asia. Despite these challenges, Marston's determination and resilience allowed her to find ways to overcome the obstacles. She credits her immigrant experiences as playing a significant role in shaping her understanding of transformative resilience and fueling her commitment to helping others navigate challenges.

Through her journey, Marston developed a deep sense of compassion for the experiences of immigrants from diverse backgrounds. She acknowledges that while she had certain privileges as a White-identifying woman with a Jewish background, she recognized immigrants' struggles and lack of privilege. Living in a highly immigrant-dominated community in London, she witnessed the strength and resilience of individuals facing unique immigration experiences.

Her experience, like Rebecca's mother, highlights the lack of control and uncertainty that immigrants often feel and face along with the pressure to meet specific criteria to remain in a country. This experience forges resilience.

Working for a resilient leader offers numerous benefits, impacting both individual employees and the organization. Resilient leaders easily navigate challenges, maintain effectiveness, and inspire their teams. They demonstrate adaptability, flexibility, and creative problem-solving.

Resilient leaders manage stress effectively, preventing burnout and ensuring sustained productivity.

Three ways immigrants build resilience within teams and organizations:

1. **THEY INCREASE MOTIVATION AND ENGAGEMENT:** Resilient leaders can often inspire and motivate their teams through perseverance and determination. When employees see their leader overcoming obstacles and continuing to push forward, it can encourage them to do the same, leading to higher levels of motivation and engagement.

2. **THEY IMPROVE PROBLEM-SOLVING:** Resilient leaders are often skilled at finding creative solutions to problems and are more capable of staying calm and focused in the face of adversity. This can create a culture of problem-solving and innovation within the team or organization, leading to better outcomes and increased productivity.

3. **THEY INCREASE JOB SATISFACTION:** When employees feel supported by a resilient leader who can guide them through difficult times, it can lead to increased job satisfaction and a sense of purpose in their work. This can lead to lower turnover rates and a more committed and engaged workforce.

The leadership landscape has undergone significant shifts in recent years, partly catalyzed by the global pandemic's impact on the economy. During the boom days, leadership primarily revolved around driving sales, developing business, and meeting the demands of a thriving economy. Many leaders relied on intrinsic skills focused on motivation and, at times, a ruthless pursuit of year-on-year sales growth, leading to an authoritarian leadership style.

Today, the communities we live and work in face unprecedented challenges—climate change, economic uncertainty, income inequality, multicultural relations, geopolitical unrest, and more. People are stressed, confused, anxious, and on edge. Navigating these complex dynamics requires a different kind of leader.

In the current leadership landscape, skills beyond technical expertise are paramount. Leaders need to embody ImmiGRIT. For instance, imagine a top-performing sales professional with extensive experience and influential connections. While their business development proficiency is undeniable, possessing versatile skills enhances their ability to collaborate with the senior leadership team in shaping the organization's strategy.

Armed with adaptability, a leader seamlessly adjusts to evolving circumstances, working collaboratively with the senior leadership team to refine the organization's strategic direction. Their resourcefulness becomes invaluable when collaborating with the HR department to facilitate the seamless adaptation of roles within their team. Instead of solely focusing on business development, this leader allocates substantial time to motivate and counsel their team, showcasing resilience in the face of challenges and contributing to a positive team dynamic.

This scenario exemplifies the contemporary leadership landscape needed for today's global marketplace. Technical competence alone is insufficient. Leaders must cultivate a skill set like the skills embodied with ImmiGRIT—adaptability, resourcefulness, and resilience. These qualities enable effective strategic decision-making and address fluid challenges within their teams. The shift toward valuing such versatile skills is important in fostering immigrant leadership.

Now that we understand ImmiGRIT, let's move on to harnessing it.

CHAPTER 9

HARNESSING IMMIGRIT

Harness /verb/ to make use of something to produce energy

Raise your hand if you've ever heard the phrase, "When in Rome, do as the Romans." This idiom is often used to encourage people to act like the locals. The first time I heard it, I was about twelve years old and on a family vacation. Our family took a ten-hour road trip from Lagos, located in the southwestern portion of Nigeria, where we lived at the time, to Jos, located in the north-central portion of Nigeria. Sitting in a restaurant, my father, the most adventurous sampler of new cuisines in the family, attempted to persuade us to try a local dish—shredded ram meat. My likely disapproving expression prompted the person serving the dish to quip, "Hey, when in Rome..." My dad promptly finished the phrase: "...do as the Romans." Sensing confusion, my dad explained that the idiom encourages individuals to try new things.

From that moment on, I have associated the idiom "When in Rome..." with persuasion. I have used it to convince friends to indulge in tapas in Barcelona, to hike the Swiss Alps to new heights, and to raft through the challenging terrains of the River Nile. I have even used it to persuade my children to try frog legs in Istanbul. I thought the only way to use that idiom was for persuasion.

That changed when a colleague used it to dissuade me from pursuing an idea. About four years into my engineering career, I transitioned from product engineering to production engineering. I shifted from designing products to redesigning production processes for some of the same products I was designing. I also moved from a production facility in Old Town, Maine, to a different facility in Bellemont, Arizona. During a discussion with my colleague about my thoughts on a production redesign, I suggested a different configuration of production staffing based on a similar process I had seen in the Old Town facility. Disagreeing with the idea, my colleague blurted out, "Hey, that may have worked there, but when in Rome..."

It took a moment to realize that my colleague was vetoing my idea based on the belief that the people in the Bellemont, Arizona, facility would not embrace it. Suddenly, someone was employing an idiom I'd always used to encourage exploration and local experiences to prevent me from pursuing an idea that didn't align with the locals' mindset. I was annoyed by the exchange and was more convinced that the idiom "When in Rome..." should be used to persuade indulgence in an extra glass of wine or feasting on carbs while on travel, not to dictate or force assimilation.

Assimilation is the process through which an individual or group embraces the cultural norms and values of the dominant society, often at the expense of their cultural heritage. It entails immigrants relinquishing their native cultural and linguistic characteristics to integrate into the broader society. This involves conforming to the expectations of the dominant group and letting go of aspects of one's culture. Assimilation is essentially a one-way journey where immigrants are expected to relinquish their cultural identity and fully adopt the cultural norms of the new society.

Assimilation is essentially a one-way journey where immigrants are expected to relinquish their cultural identity and fully adopt the cultural norms of the new society.

In contrast, as we've discussed, adaptability is the capacity to adjust to new situations and circumstances while retaining one's cultural identity. It means being open and flexible to new experiences and learning from them, all while maintaining a sense of one's culture and identity. Adaptability is a two-way process that involves both the immigrant and the host society making adjustments and accommodations to each other.

Immigrants are expected to assimilate with the dominant culture quickly—a process metaphorically described as the melting pot theory, or more candidly, assimilation. While adapting is fundamental when relating to a culture different from our own, one's character, values, and personality are essential, and they should not change just because you are in a new country. The workplace environment should allow individuals to bring their ideas and consciously decide which aspects they are willing to let go of and which factors are nonnegotiable and integral parts of who they have chosen to be.

For instance, when my parents visit me from Nigeria, they make concessions on their clothing to draw less attention to themselves. They are not fans of American food, so they choose other types of food. They adapt their clothing to align with the culture while consciously making choices about their food preferences rather than simply melting into the pot.

If you've ever dined at the chain restaurant Melting Pot, you will understand the concept of melting into a pot. It's a dining experience where a blend of cheeses, liquid, and seasoning is added and gently stirred until melted, creating a cheese fondue mixture. Then, the fondue mixture is enjoyed by dipping bread and vegetables into the cheese or fruit into a chocolate fondue. In a broader sense, Melting Pot serves as a metaphor for different cultural elements "melting together" into a common culture—a monoculture, so to speak.

The "melting pot" metaphor gained popularity following the play titled *The Melting Pot* by Israel Zangwill, which premiered in Washington in 1908 during the peak of European immigration to the US.[1] The play, closely based on William Shakespeare's *Romeo and Juliet*, unfolds in New York City, the home of many new US immigrants at the time. It narrates the story of David, a recent Jewish immigrant from Russia, who falls in love with a Christian Greek-Orthodox Russian girl, overcoming prejudice between their respective communities in America. David grapples with ways to reconcile his faith while being conscious of the extraordinary suffering of new immigrants arriving daily. Meanwhile, the cast of immigrants poses the question, "Who shall we be?" as life unfolds around them through the aspirations of the young and the suffering of their elders.

Even at the time when Zangwill's play opened in Washington, many opposed the idea that America was a melting pot into which immigrants from different races and cultures could seamlessly assimilate or that they would want to lose their own ethnic and cultural identities. Not only is there no objective measure of assimilation, but there is no timeline either. And there shouldn't be. As Laila Lalami aptly concludes in her 2017 *New York Times* article, "What Does It Take to 'Assimilate' in America?" "One reason immigration is continuously debated in America is that there is no consensus on whether assimilation should be about national principles or national identity."[2] And there you have it!

Adaptability, not assimilation, should be the goal in our workplaces. This way, we can capitalize on the unique perspectives of immigrants as they take on new information or experiences and incorporate them into their existing ideas. That's the magic of adaptability and the perils of expecting assimilation on a timeline other than the one to which the immigrant is willing to yield.

CREATE A STEW

The day I became a naturalized US citizen, my then four-year-old daughter happily declared, "Yaaaaay, you are an American like the rest of the family now."

As callous and as simplistic as my four-year-old's statement that day may have been, I think this sentiment reflects the perspective of many leaders within the workplace—this "Hurry up and become American" sentiment. It's treated like a light switch to be turned on and left on as if the other parts of what immigrants bring do not matter. We also see this callousness with our diversity, equity, and inclusion (DEI) efforts. There is a disregard for the intersectionality that makes up an immigrant's whole being. What is not seen, not acknowledged, and often not recognized is how being an immigrant impacts one's experiences.

Before the day I took the Oath of Allegiance at my naturalization ceremony to become a US citizen, I had already been in the country for eighteen years. During that time, I experienced culture shock, learned new customs, built new social networks, picked up a different accent, and persevered. As an immigrant, you often feel like you're neither part of your native country anymore nor part of where you are. So the day I became a US citizen, I felt like all I did was make my two parts official—Nigerian and American, both equally me.

Instead of creating a melting pot, how about we make a stew? The honorable Judge Dan Aaron Polster, currently the senior district judge of the United States District Court for the Northern District of Ohio, presided over my naturalization ceremony. I took my oath with about fifty other people. Taking the Oath of Allegiance is mandatory as the final step of the naturalization process. I have always held on to what Judge Polster said that day about creating a stew before he administered the oath.

> He said, "It's more accurate to call the United States a deep, delicious stew instead of a melting pot. Many families have special recipes for their family stew; when made correctly, you can taste every ingredient and individual spice. And that's what each of you is doing today, adding in your special spice, because in this country, we are all

immigrants, making something greater than we could ever do by ourselves."

Creating a stew means including employees' insights from various cultural backgrounds. Inevitably, after many years in a country, immigrants become more like natives while maintaining their culture. In America, they become football fans, eat hamburgers, and watch fireworks on the Fourth of July while maintaining connections with their countries of origin, as has been the case for me. They may come to see themselves as hyphenated Americans, but Americans nonetheless. I am Nigerian-American—culturally Nigerian, nationally American.

To create a stew, our workplaces need to establish an infrastructure that can harness ImmiGRIT to unlock the superpowers of immigrant leadership. When you harness something, you bring it under your control and use it. That involves developing a system. As a mechanical engineer, I learned how to apply the principles of physics, mathematics, and material science to design, analyze, and manufacture systems and devices. The systems were designed to harness energy by capturing available energy and converting it to electrical power.

In that vein, through my research, I have unraveled the system for harnessing ImmiGRIT. It revolves around three essential components: cultural competence, curious conversations, and continuous progress.

A. CULTURAL COMPETENCE

Culture is a set of shared traditions, beliefs, customs, and the history of a group of people. It forms a system of rules that shapes who we are and influences how we express ourselves as part of a group and as individuals. We all develop some culture, and our environment determines what we learn, how we know it, and the rules for living with others. These rules are transmitted from one generation to the next and one leader to the next, sometimes adapted to the times. At other times, they are coined traditions and need a clearer understanding of who continues to benefit from them.

A few years ago, I attended a community theater performance of *Fiddler on the Roof*, a production that held the record for the longest-running Broadway musical for almost a decade.[3] The musical, published in 1964, revolves around Tevye, a poor Jewish milkman with five daughters in a Russian settlement, the village of Anatevka. Tevye attempts to maintain his Jewish religious and cultural traditions as outside influences encroach upon his family's lives. The story unfolds as he copes with the strong-willed actions of his three older daughters, who wish to marry for love rather than following the tradition of being paired by a matchmaker.

The show begins with a fiddler on a roof playing the opening song "Tradition." In this song, Tevye explains the roles of each social class—the fathers, the mothers, the sons, and the daughters—in the village of Anatevka. He describes how the traditional roles of each, along with people like the matchmaker, the beggar, and the rabbi, contribute to the village. As the play progresses, each scene balances how villagers try to continue their traditions and keep their society running while the world around them changes. Tevye is repeatedly confronted with the question of who the tradition serves as culture evolves.

While traditions shape how people live and develop sensitivity and respect for others' belief systems and societal norms, culture evolves in response to societal changes or external influences from historical events, rituals, or beliefs. Like societies, organizations have a culture defined by policies, procedures, programs, and processes, incorporating specific values, beliefs, assumptions, and customs. However, an organizational culture may not inherently promote cultural competence. A culturally competent organization transforms knowledge about different groups of people into standards, policies, and practices that facilitate harmony and effectiveness.

Harnessing ImmiGRIT starts with building a culturally competent organization.

Cultural competence is crucial today more than ever before as the cultural make-up of communities has changed. Over the last decade, immigrants and refugees from Central and South America, Africa, Eastern Europe, and the former Soviet Union have come to the US seeking refuge, asylum, and opportunity. Global migration has increased similarly. Regardless of the reasons behind one's decision to migrate, their arrival brings increased cultural diversity and, in some cases, cultural misunderstandings and confusion.

Building a culturally competent organization means changing how people think about other cultures, how they communicate, and how they operate. An organization's structure, leadership, and activities must reflect many traditions, values, perspectives, styles, and priorities. A culturally competent organization can bring many different behaviors, attitudes, and policies into its system to work effectively in cross-cultural settings, producing better outcomes.

A culturally competent organization should also emphasize the advantages of cultural diversity, celebrate the contributions of each culture, encourage the positive outcomes of interacting with many cultures, and support the sharing of power among people from different cultures through its leaders. A culturally competent organization is where immigrants thrive, becoming empowered as leaders.

Becoming a culturally competent organization focuses on aligning leadership, policies, and practices with goals. Everyone should be involved in cultural intelligence training and creating systems and processes that preserve and transmit cultural knowledge within an organization. This involvement enriches our workplace, encourages creativity and innovation, and improves profit.

CULTURAL INTELLIGENCE TRAINING BUILDS THE CULTURAL COMPETENCE OF AN ORGANIZATION

You've likely heard about your intelligence quotient (IQ) and emotional intelligence quotient (EQ), but have you heard of the cultural intelligence quotient (CQ)? If asked about your CQ, what do you think it would be? Do you know what it takes to build CQ and how it can benefit your organization?

In their book *Handbook of Cultural Intelligence*, Ang and Van Dyne define cultural intelligence as an individual's capability to function effectively across national, ethnic, and even organizational cultures.[4] However, CQ is not merely a catchphrase for cultural sensitivity. It is not a list of dos and don'ts learned online or in some book about interacting with someone from another culture. Rooted in research, CQ is proven to enhance the effectiveness of leaders as they seek to meet the demands of our increasingly globalized world. Culture profoundly shapes how we do our work, and with cultural intelligence, you can develop a skill set that can be applied to any cross-cultural scenario. This, in turn, creates pathways to leadership for immigrant talent and enables opportunities for business growth.

In an increasingly diverse business environment, leaders must possess a high CQ to navigate the thicket of habits, gestures, and assumptions that define employee differences. Foreign cultures are not limited to other countries but exist within corporations and communities. Interacting with individuals, especially immigrants, demands CQ.

What corporations gain from authentically embracing immigrants depends on how well corporations and their employees understand the relevance of CQ in allowing people to unleash their true potential by simply being themselves. Leaders with high CQ can only thrive within a culturally competent organization.

DEI TRAINING MUST INCLUDE CULTURAL INTELLIGENCE
The past few years have witnessed a reenvisioning of diversity, equity, and inclusion (DEI). Almost every institution has incorporated a DEI program or training—from universities to healthcare to the corporate world. A critical part of this programming is bias training, addressing how conscious and unconscious judgments affect our treatment of others.

While perceptions around characteristics like gender, race, religion, etc., have often been addressed in these training sessions, immigrants are not a lens we typically consider in the conversation. DEI training tends to overemphasize bias training rather than developing employees' cultural competence, enabling them to navigate and appreciate diverse cultures, customs, and traditions.

At this point, you might wonder, *How can my organization build a supportive infrastructure that addresses the distinctive needs of immigrants?* To truly change, an organization must commit to continued programming, evaluation, and creating an inclusive environment for all cultures. Organizations should integrate cultural knowledge into every facet by identifying the cultural knowledge that needs to be incorporated, including traditional practices, stories, beliefs, and values.

Once identified, organizations should document cultural knowledge in a clear and accessible format and train staff to effectively utilize the gained knowledge. Policies should be responsive to cultural diversity, and program materials should reflect positive images of all cultures. The most critical actions to be conscious of are usually the ones we take for granted. For instance, physical distance during social interactions varies by culture. If a staff member routinely touches the arm of whomever she is talking to, some cultures might misread this. Organization members can avoid such miscommunication if the organization undergoes cultural self-assessment.

Alongside all employees trained in cultural intelligence, leaders must have the skills to navigate cross-cultural interactions effectively. This is how organizations sustain cultural competence.

B. CURIOUS CONVERSATIONS

Communication is at the core of cross-cultural interactions. Leaders must be adept at conveying messages clearly and respectfully, considering linguistic nuances, nonverbal cues, and variations in communication styles. This ability is encapsulated in the concept of curious conversations.

Can you think about a time you felt seen and valued at work? Chances are, it was following a curious conversation.

Imagine this conversation:

> **Manager**: Hey, I've been thinking about ways to better serve our Spanish-speaking clients, and I know you speak Spanish fluently. Do you have any suggestions?

> **Immigrant Employee**: One idea could be translating some of our materials, such as our website or brochures, into Spanish. Having someone on the team who can speak Spanish and communicate directly with our clients could also be helpful.

> **Manager**: Those are both great suggestions. Would you be interested in taking on that role as our Spanish-speaking liaison?

> **Immigrant Employee**: Yes, I would love to. It would be an excellent opportunity to use my language skills and help our clients feel more comfortable and understood.

Manager: That's fantastic. I'm glad we can work together to serve our clients better and create a more inclusive workplace. Thank you for bringing this up and offering your expertise.

This example demonstrates a curious conversation. Notice the manager's curiosity and openness to ideas about better serving clients by recognizing the immigrant employee's language skills and offering an expertise-aligned role. This is the difference between a conversation that makes you feel awkward and othered versus one that makes you feel seen and valued. The employee feels valued and appreciated, not tokenized for their unique skills and contributions, and the company benefits from better serving its Spanish-speaking clients.

Overall, the curious conversation helps not only all employees but particularly immigrants in building better pathways to their leadership. As an added benefit, this conversation builds stronger teams and improves business outcomes.

A curious conversation is more than mere dialogue; it's an exploration and a learning opportunity. In this dynamic exchange, both parties actively seek to understand a topic, ask questions, and share ideas. This type of dialogue creates a sense of wonder, openness, and a genuine desire to acquire new knowledge and insights.

To have a curious conversation, be N-I-C-E:

NONJUDGMENTAL: Avoid making value judgments about the other person's beliefs or experiences. Keep an open mind, a willingness to listen, and a readiness to learn.

INFORMAL: Allow your conversations to unfold in various settings—from casual coffee shop chats to walks between meetings—breaking away from strict formats or formal rules.

COURTEOUS: Be polite and respectful during the conversation despite potentially covering controversial topics. The goal is learning, not agreement, so actively listen to each other's opinions and perspectives.

ENGAGING: Keep the conversation dynamic and engaging by contributing to the conversation, posing questions, sharing ideas, and building upon each other's thoughts.

In recent years, the discussion around immigration has grown increasingly contentious, seeping into workplace discussions and transforming them into pitched debates. Sometimes, people shy away from the conversation altogether. However, as a society, we lose when emotionally charged topics like immigration become off-limits, hindering the exploration and bridging of diverse opinions. This is particularly important when these discussions directly impact the lives of specific groups of people. Without constructive engagement, the immigration debate lingers without resolution, imposing severe consequences on immigrants, their families, and the many Americans whose lives intersect with those of immigrants through work.

Curious conversations, especially those involving immigrants, offer significant benefits. They P-R-O-B-E:

PROMOTE UNDERSTANDING: Curiosity provides a pathway to better understand different cultures and perspectives. By posing questions about immigrants' experiences, individuals gain insights into their lives, struggles, and achievements, fostering empathy and mutual respect.

REDUCE STEREOTYPES: Immigrants often face stereotypes and misconceptions that lead to discrimination. Curious conversations challenge these stereotypes and dispel myths by providing accurate information and personal experiences.

OVERCOME BARRIERS: Curiosity is a powerful tool for breaking down barriers, hindering integration and understanding. By actively seeking to learn about immigrants' experiences, individuals can identify and address systemic challenges.

BUILD CONNECTIONS: Curiosity becomes a tool for building connections between immigrants and nonimmigrants, creating opportunities to find common ground. Individuals can discover potential collaborations, business ventures, and cultural exchanges that enrich communities and contribute to collective growth and prosperity.

ENCOURAGE INTEGRATION: Curious conversations act as bridges, providing opportunities for immigrants to share their cultures and traditions while enabling nonimmigrants to learn and appreciate them.

MASTERING THE ART OF CURIOUS CONVERSATIONS STARTS WITH ASKING HOW, NOT WHY

Mónica Guzmán, a liberal journalist and daughter of Mexican immigrants who voted for Donald Trump twice, recognized the potential of curiosity in overcoming the deep political divides between her and her family. In her book, *I Never Thought of It That Way: How to Have Fearlessly Curious Conversations in Dangerously Divided Times*, Guzmán shares the tools needed for curious conversations, with a fundamental principle emphasizing asking how instead of why.[5]

Guzmán explains the significance of focusing on how in an enlightening TEDx talk—in situations rife with fear and mistrust, asking why may come across as demanding justification, forcing individuals to prove their worth before being heard, and by contrast, asking how invites people to share their personal stories. It invites them to walk you down the path they took to their views and allows you to walk right alongside them.[6]

To start a curious conversation, ask how someone came to believe or understand something, not why. Most of us start a conversation trying to change people's minds or get them to buy into our idea, making it impossible to understand them and hindering the essence of curiosity.

For immigrants to ascend to leadership roles, corporations must foster environments where leaders and teams can communicate effectively, learn from diverse perspectives, and understand experiences different from their own. This forms the secret sauce for stretching, disrupting, and growing, allowing collaborative innovation to flourish.

Once a culturally competent organization is established through comprehensive cultural competency training, and leaders are equipped with the skills for curious conversations, understanding the unconscious biases faced by immigrants discussed in chapter 5 and how those impact their ability to contribute to organizational leadership becomes more intuitive.

C. CONTINUOUS PROGRESS

Establishing a workplace system that harnesses ImmiGRIT is a transformative journey that also requires a commitment to a system of tracking progress. Measuring a system is the only way to know if it is working. The most effective systems are those with established metrics and key performance indicators (KPIs) to track progress.

It's impossible to improve at anything that is not tracked. Establishing key performance indicators (KPIs) within systems allows for the monitoring of progress. Tracking immigrant representation in leadership should be the same. Effective systems for increasing immigrant representation in leadership roles should rely on well-defined metrics.

Follow these seven steps to establish and track relevant metrics:

1) BASELINE MEASUREMENT

Begin by establishing a baseline measurement of the current representation of immigrants in leadership roles. Initial data provide reference points for tracking progress, breaking down the information by leadership levels, departments, and other pertinent categories.

2) IMMIGRANT RECRUITMENT METRICS

Track metrics related to immigrant recruitment:

- Consider the percentage of immigrant candidates in the hiring pool. Measure the proportion of immigrant candidates in the applicant pool for leadership positions.
- Consider immigrant recruitment success rate. Evaluate the success rate of immigrant candidates securing leadership positions.

3) PROMOTION AND SUCCESSION PLANNING

Assess the fairness of promotion and succession planning processes:

- Consider the percentage of immigrants in leadership development programs. Track the participation of immigrants in programs designed to nurture leadership skills.
- Consider succession planning effectiveness. Evaluate the representation of immigrants in the pipeline for leadership positions.

4) LEADERSHIP ACCOUNTABILITY

Ensure leadership accountability for diversity and inclusion goals through metrics:

- Consider the percentage of leadership performance evaluations tied to diversity goals. Incorporate diversity and inclusion metrics into leadership performance evaluations.
- Consider leadership commitment to diversity initiatives. Assess leadership engagement and commitment to fostering a diverse and inclusive workplace.

5) EMPLOYEE FEEDBACK AND ENGAGEMENT

Gather feedback from employees to assess workplace inclusivity:

- Consider employee satisfaction survey results. Analyze survey results to understand immigrant employees' satisfaction levels with the organization's diversity and inclusion efforts.
- Consider the inclusion index. Develop an index considering factors like belonging, representation, and support for immigrant employees.

6) MONITORING AND COMMUNICATION

Establish dashboards or reports providing a visual representation of critical metrics and KPIs. Implement a communication plan to share updates regularly with leadership, employees, and stakeholders.

- Review and refine metrics and KPIs regularly based on evolving organizational needs and industry standards. Solicit employee feedback, assess the impact of diversity initiatives, and adjust goals accordingly. This iterative approach ensures continuous improvement and alignment with organizational objectives.

With this robust framework, organizations can comprehensively track progress in increasing immigrant representation in leadership roles, fostering continuous improvement and ensuring alignment with diversity and inclusion goals.

* * *

Engineers build systems to harness energy in many ways. They capture solar, wind, and water energy and use them to power microgrids and electric vehicles. For my leaders reading this, I have engineered you a system to harness ImmiGRIT through the three Cs—the three essential components: Cultural Competence, Curious Conversations, and Continuous Progress. As a leader, your responsibility is to build them out. The desire to conserve energy, reduce greenhouse gases, and promote a sustainable energy system drives an engineer's desire to harness energy from natural resources. In the same way, the desire to propel innovation, increase profits, and revolutionize workplace culture should drive your willingness to harness ImmiGRIT.

Now that we've established a system to harness ImmiGRIT, let's move on to cultivating it.

CHAPTER 10

CULTIVATING IMMIGRIT

Cultivate /verb/ to develop and improve something.

I have a house plant that has lived with me in seven homes, four cities, and two states. Despite lacking a green thumb and unlike some of my past botanical casualties, this plant survives and thrives. I've realized it is also the only plant for which I have established a relocation system.

Upon reaching a new home, regardless of its configuration, I instinctively place the plant diagonally across a large window, slightly elevated. Once situated, I maintain practices that contribute to its growth—regular watering, periodic nutrient additions, and a gentle rotation to ensure all sides bask in the sunlight.

The key insight here is that a system is only effective if you can cultivate the benefits derived from it. Cultivating ImmiGRIT involves nurturing, refining, and developing the harnessed elements discussed in the previous chapter.

I will not belabor the points already discussed regarding immigrants assuming leadership positions, having shown how they encounter personal challenges and systemic barriers. Navigating these obstacles requires immigrants to acknowledge their unique skills and competencies. Simultaneously, institutions, corporations, and communities must actively empower immigrant leaders.

For immigrants aspiring to leadership roles, relying solely on their skills and expertise falls short. The systemic barriers imposed by the traditional archetype of a leader hinder their progress. Addressing those challenges requires proactive steps to cultivate and support immigrant leaders, and this begins with allowing the diverse experiences immigrants bring to flourish. Moreover, organizations should reimagine leadership development programs to accommodate immigrant leaders' unique needs and backgrounds. Sponsorship initiatives also play a vital role in helping immigrants navigate their careers alongside leaders who can advocate for their advancement.

RECOGNIZING IMMIGRANT LEADERSHIP POTENTIAL

While working as a full-time mechanical engineer for a prominent global Fortune 500 company, I dedicated myself to earning an MBA, specializing in finance and strategy. Upon completing my MBA, I was eager to utilize my enhanced skill set within the corporate strategy group of my then employer and applied for an open leadership role.

With great enthusiasm, I approached my boss to share news about the role I had applied for, but my excitement was met with a sobering response. My boss expressed concern, noting that replacing my engineering position would be more challenging than finding someone for the corporate strategy role. He believed it was mutually beneficial for me to stay in an engineering role, especially considering the company's effort in securing and sponsoring my H-1B visa. The H-1B nonimmigrant visa program allows employers to employ immigrants in specialty occupations, and because it is tied to an employer, an H-1B employee is limited to opportunities within the sponsoring company.

I did not get the job. I was devastated. I felt underutilized, my potential wasted. Instead, the company promoted me to the position of engineering manager. While managing a team of engineers was an honor, it lacked how I envisioned utilizing my MBA. The new role offered no involvement in strategy and no exposure to finance. It felt like a missed opportunity. It is not enough to acknowledge qualifications on paper; organizations must strategically deploy immigrant talent to areas where their skills align and contribute meaningfully. This involves a comprehensive understanding of individual strengths, experiences, and aspirations.

An estimated 47.4 percent of the foreign-born population who arrived in the US from 2010 to 2019 have a bachelor's degree or higher, compared to 36.3 percent of native-born Americans.[1] Yet it is estimated that immigrants start with wages 17 percent below those of native born Americans.[2] According to economist Barry Chiswick, immigrants must work ten to fifteen years to close the wage gap, depending on their country of origin.[3] The failure of organizations to fully utilize immigrant talent is not only costing immigrants their earning potential but also impacting profitability.

Picture an immigrant professional with a background in international business, not merely acknowledged for their expertise but actively immersed in projects demanding a global perspective. This alignment fosters a profound sense of purpose for the employee and propels the organization forward through enriched decision-making. Reflecting on a personal anecdote shared by an old colleague, Tania Klein, amplifies the significance of this narrative. She convinced her leaders to go beyond recognizing her technical skills and embrace her leadership skills. However, identifying and elevating leadership should not fall on individuals alone.

Today, Tania Klein holds the esteemed position of assistant vice president of corporate finance and business decision support at a leading automotive glass and insurance claims management company. Her remarkable journey as a Bengali immigrant to the US, driven by a quest for higher education, unfolds from her early days in a technical role as an accountant sponsored by her former company through an H-1B visa. From those initial footsteps, Klein now steers a team of ten at an entirely different organization.

In the initial chapters of her career, Tania immersed herself in the relentless demands of number crunching and the meticulous preparation of accounting reports. Despite a sense of camaraderie with colleagues, she soon outgrew the confines of her role, yearning for exposure to more diverse work. Tethered to this routine and equally feeling underutilized due to her H-1B sponsorship, Tania came to a pivotal realization for immigrants.

She told me, "You really need to put yourself out there, and it may sound cliché, but once you believe you're a leader, you can't give up on seeking it."

Yet the proficiency in her role, once lauded as a strength, was a confining label. Even when invited to tables where discussions unfolded about product launches or strategic planning, Tania found herself relegated to the role of a number cruncher. As she recalled that phase of her career, she remembered the subtle whispers that persisted, *I am more than this.* The challenge lay in conveying this realization to others, a subtle dance of, "I'm technical, but I want to do more," familiar to many immigrants who outgrow the roles that initially brought them through the door. How does one articulate the depth of their capabilities, and once communicated, how does an organization support that development?

Tania's journey of convincing was marked by numerous failures and persistent attempts to express the vastness of her potential. Ultimately, her potential was seen and embraced by her leader. However, the narrative extends beyond individual triumphs. Establishing platforms for showcasing skills like internal events, knowledge-sharing sessions, and cross-functional collaboration projects can serve as powerful catalysts.

In the corporate landscape, many immigrants find themselves confined to middle management. Despite excelling in their technical roles, these middle managers often need more resources and support to ascend to the next leadership level. According to Harvey J. Coleman in his book *Empowering Yourself: The Organizational Game Revealed*, success is often determined by factors that go beyond just job performance.[4] Coleman asserts that performance, image, and exposure (PIE) determine career success. He emphasizes that performance is most important early in one's career, but exposure becomes increasingly important as individuals aim for executive-level positions. The more contentious and possibly unsettling aspects of Coleman's conclusions revolve around the weightings placed on these elements: Performance counts for 10 percent of one's success, image 30 percent, and exposure an eye-popping 60 percent.[5]

Although the book was published in 1996, its implications still resonate today. If all an immigrant does is perform their job well without gaining exposure to a broad array of the "right" stakeholders, they fall short. So, how do immigrants get exposure?

Reflecting on my own experiences managing technical teams, I can confirm the accuracy of Coleman's PIE model. In management discussions I've been involved in regarding promotions and succession planning, someone in the room typically puts forth a candidate's name for consideration. My first thoughts aren't usually about whether the candidate performs the job well (I assume so). Instead, I immediately wonder what I know about them (exposure).

If I don't know anything about the person, I tend to say nothing or push back for more information about them (again, exposure). The final litmus test generally involves discussions surrounding the candidate's image. If the team views the person as a capable, consistent, positive change agent, it's typically a done deal.

While personal accountability is integral to the PIE concept, emphasizing exposure in leadership decisions means leaders play a pivotal role in helping others get noticed. This is especially significant for immigrant professionals, given they have to build entirely new social networks. Immigrants have unique exposure needs, and we need leaders to play their part in bridging that gap.

RETHINK LEADERSHIP DEVELOPMENT

American football has always intrigued me, not just for its rules that often elude my understanding but also because of an observation that made headlines in an NBC News article published in September 2020, which read, "Most NFL Players Are Black. So Why Aren't There More Black Head Coaches?" That season began with only three Black head coaches out of the thirty-two NFL teams in a league where the players are roughly 70 percent Black.[6] The disparity begs a critical *why*?

I propose a theory to unravel this perplexing issue. Coaching development programs appear to overlook or neglect Black candidates. If playing is a presumed prerequisite for coaching, that doesn't seem to translate into proportional representation for Black coaches despite the majority of players being Black. Effective leadership programs should mirror the diverse demographic of leaders they aim to cultivate. The significance of leadership development programs in sculpting and nurturing leaders cannot be overstated. Companies that actively engage in such programs empower leaders to acquire the indispensable knowledge, support, and confidence required to excel in their careers and guide their organizations and communities. However, there's a caveat. These programs must address the distinct challenges and opportunities encountered by the leaders they seek to develop.

Before crafting leadership development programs, it's essential to understand the unique challenges immigrant leaders face. For instance, an immigrant leader might find themselves in a position where their leadership style, which may be effective in their home country, requires adaptation to better align with cultural expectations.

Recognizing these challenges is the foundational step in designing effective leadership development initiatives. The effectiveness of leadership development programs lies in their ability to go beyond generic leadership training.

Leadership development programs that facilitate exposure to senior executives and industry leaders offer the most significant value to immigrants. Immigrant professionals often need more access to influential networks and opportunities. By providing platforms for interaction with established leaders, these programs help bridge the gap and expose immigrant leaders to valuable insights, career opportunities, and industry trends. Immigrant leaders can gain visibility and recognition, paving the way for advancement and increased leadership responsibilities.

Networking is another component of leadership development programs that benefits immigrants more proportionately. These programs often bring together a diverse group of immigrant professionals from various industries, sectors, and backgrounds. Immigrants can connect, share experiences, and build relationships with fellow leaders through networking activities. These connections provide a robust support system and create opportunities for collaboration, knowledge sharing, and future partnerships.

Organizations, professional associations, educational institutions, and community organizations can offer leadership development programs. They can be structured courses, workshops, conferences, or long-term programs that combine various elements of training, mentorship, and networking. Whatever the forum and how it is delivered, immigrant professionals need access to leadership training programs tailored to the immigrant experience.

The landscape of leadership development programs demands a transformative shift. There needs to be more than a one-size-fits-all approach. I vividly recall when leadership training centered around crafting performance reviews or time management—aspects that offer limited assistance to immigrant leaders. According to April Whitson, a global human resources manager for an electrical equipment company and author of the book *The STAY Challenge: A Leader's Guide to Managing Unwanted Turnover & Regrettable Retention*, she believes that the evolution in leadership development has been marked by a significant shift toward teaching leaders the art of adapting to diverse personalities. "It's how to build a culture where employees don't want to leave," Whitson believes. This shift holds immense potential for immigrant professionals, providing a pathway to fortify their leadership skills and surmount barriers.

Furthermore, organizations should go beyond conventional approaches. Providing opportunities for immigrant leaders to immerse themselves in cross-functional projects is essential. Such engagements broaden perspectives and serve as catalysts for enhancing leadership capabilities. Also, consider crafting cross-cultural collaboration projects. It could be a powerful way for immigrant leaders to showcase their skills and insights while fostering understanding and collaboration among diverse teams.

Even if an organization operates solely nationally without global reach, the benefits of highlighting cross-cultural competence remain substantial. I have personally led workshops that simulate cross-cultural collaboration and customer service interactions, creating scenarios with a diverse customer base. This approach offers meaningful opportunities for leaders to exhibit their capabilities. It's a feasible and effective strategy, even for organizations with a purely national focus.

The underlying message here is that leadership development must be dynamic, tailored, and geared toward equipping leaders, especially immigrants, with the adaptability and skills needed for today's diverse and dynamic professional landscape.

In our insightful conversation, Whitson and I discussed the prevalent challenge organizations encounter when embracing and nurturing leaders from diverse cultural backgrounds. As Whitson explains, the inherent difficulty for organizations, hiring managers, and HR teams lies in the hesitancy to take risks by placing individuals who may not initially align with the prevailing organizational culture. This process demands considerable time for cultural integration. It explains why there is an inclination to opt for the easier route—hiring individuals who seamlessly fit in and require less time for development, coaching, and mentorship.

To navigate these challenges, Whitson advocates for a proactive approach, challenging organizations to resist the allure of the easy road. Drawing on a personal example involving hiring an immigrant general manager for a factory in a rural community, candid discussions about cultural differences were integral during the interviewing and selection processes. April believes that investing time up front in communication about the cultural differences during the selection process and having local mentors to guide and support immigrant leaders in navigating unfamiliar territories sets the stage for addressing the challenges that may arise.

A pivotal aspect highlighted in my conversation with Whitson is the need for organizations to create a support system of mentors and sponsors for immigrant leaders, a fundamental component in ensuring the success and acceptance of immigrant leaders within the organization.

MENTORING PROGRAMS

To understand the different career trajectories between White and minority executives, David Thomas conducted a study on the progression of racial minorities at three large US corporations. He documented his research findings in an article, "The Truth about Mentoring Minorities: Race Matters." Thomas's research showed that minorities who advance the furthest shared one characteristic—a strong network of mentors and corporate sponsors. Minorities who plateaued in middle management received instructional mentoring, which helped them develop skills. By contrast, minorities who became executives enjoyed fuller developmental relationships with their mentors.[7]

Without question, mentoring programs play a vital role in nurturing and developing immigrant leaders. These programs provide a supportive framework for immigrant professionals to grow, thrive, and reach their full leadership potential. By offering guidance, advocacy, and networking opportunities, mentoring and sponsorship programs can empower immigrant leaders to overcome obstacles and excel in their careers.

Mentoring programs connect immigrant leaders with experienced professionals who can offer valuable insights, guidance, and support. Mentors are trusted advisors and role models who share their knowledge, experience, and expertise. They provide a safe space for immigrant leaders to ask questions, seek advice, and discuss challenges they may face in their professional journeys. Mentors offer encouragement and help mentees develop essential skills, such as effective communication, problem-solving, and decision-making.

In his research, Thomas offers mentors the best ways to support mentees for maximum impact, highlighting five critical dimensions:

1. They swing open doors to challenging assignments, providing growth opportunities.
2. They strategically place their mentees in high-trust positions, fostering an environment conducive to success.
3. They build trust and extend advice, drawing from their experience to guide their mentees effectively.
4. They evolve into sponsors, actively championing the career advancement of their mentor.
5. They act as a shield, offering protection against naysayers and detractors.

These are the dimensions a well-structured mentoring program benefiting immigrant leaders should have.

For immigrant leaders, having a mentor can be particularly beneficial in navigating unfamiliar work environments and cultural nuances. Mentors can offer insights into workplace dynamics, unwritten rules, and organizational politics. They can help immigrant leaders understand and adapt to the cultural expectations and norms of their new professional setting. Mentors can also guide career development, assisting immigrant leaders with setting goals, identifying growth opportunities, and charting a path toward leadership roles.

On this point, Raphael Okutoro, the coordinator of summer programs within the Division of Lifelong Learning at the University of Maine, wholeheartedly agrees. Drawing from his career journey spanning over two decades, Raphael attributes his entrance into higher education to the guidance of exceptional mentors.

Raphael's immigrant story began in 1998 when he arrived in the US after enduring a decade of separation from his family due to the Liberian Civil War. Settling in the Bronx, New York, he completed high school. He pursued his undergraduate degree, earning a Bachelor of Science in Environmental Science with a minor in Wildlife Biology at the University of Vermont (UVM). Interestingly, during his time at UVM, despite majoring in environmental science, he found himself working in the admissions office through a student job. This unexpected turn led him to discover a network of mentors, including the director of admissions at that time, whose influence played a pivotal role in shaping Raphael's career choices. Their collective impact was transformative, propelling him definitively into higher education.

To establish successful mentoring programs for immigrant leaders, organizations should ensure that these initiatives are well-structured and accessible by developing clear program guidelines, matching mentors and mentees based on their goals and compatibility, and providing resources and training for mentors to enhance their effectiveness.

SPONSORSHIP PROGRAMS

Sponsorship programs complement mentoring by providing active advocacy and support for immigrant leaders. As Thomas points out, sponsors often evolve from mentoring programs and relationships. Sponsors are influential individuals within an organization who use their position and influence to champion the advancement of their protégés. Unlike mentors, sponsors actively promote their protégés' visibility and career progression. They advocate for their protégés' inclusion in high-profile projects, assignments, and leadership opportunities. Sponsors can help immigrants build essential connections and networks, opening doors to new possibilities and enhancing their visibility within the organization.

Research from the Center for Talent Innovation reinforces the impact of sponsorship.[8] Employees enrolled in formalized sponsorship programs are 23 percent more likely to ascend within their organizations, highlighting the tangible benefits of structured sponsorship initiatives.

Sponsorship is particularly important for immigrant leaders as it can help mitigate the biases and barriers they may face in their careers. Immigrant professionals may encounter prejudice or stereotypes that can hinder their advancement. Sponsors can leverage their credibility and influence to challenge these biases and create a more inclusive and equitable environment. They can help ensure that immigrant leaders are evaluated based on their skills, qualifications, and potential rather than their cultural or linguistic background.

Organizations can formalize sponsorship programs to institutionalize sponsorship. These programs pair immigrant leaders with influential sponsors who possess the authority and influence to shape career trajectories within the company.

At its core, sponsorship is about actively dismantling barriers that may impede career progression. An immigrant leader with a dedicated sponsor is more likely to be entrusted with stretch assignments—projects that challenge their skills and capabilities. This level of advocacy serves as a catalyst, bridging the opportunity gap that immigrant leaders may face due to cultural differences or latent biases.

Both mentors and sponsors provide valuable support, but their roles differ slightly. While mentors offer guidance and advice, sponsors actively use their influence to create opportunities for their protégés. Combining these two types of support can be highly effective in accelerating the growth and development of immigrant leaders.

Mentoring and sponsorship programs are invaluable in nurturing and developing immigrant leaders. These programs provide essential guidance, support, and advocacy, enabling immigrant professionals to navigate their careers successfully and reach their leadership potential. By investing in these programs, organizations create a more inclusive and equitable environment where immigrant leaders can thrive, contribute their unique perspectives, and drive organizational success.

NETWORKING AND COMMUNITY ENGAGEMENT

Networking plays a vital role in career advancement for immigrant leaders. Organizations can support immigrant leaders by providing networking opportunities, hosting events that promote cross-cultural collaboration, and facilitating connections with industry professionals and leaders. These activities allow immigrant professionals to connect, build relationships, and expand their support networks. By actively engaging with their communities and establishing meaningful connections, immigrant leaders can enhance their visibility, access valuable resources, and contribute to their growth and the development of others.

Earlier in this book, I expressed my surprise about the limited research on immigrant leadership in corporate America. Although some studies have explored the representation of ethnic minorities in senior corporate roles, the focus on immigrant leadership talent remains scarce. Understanding immigrants' contributions as leaders and their unique paths to reach executive positions is important.

In 2017, Sami Mahroum and Rashid Ansari sought to illuminate these questions, presenting their research findings in the article "What the Data Tells Us about Immigrant Executives in the US."[9] Their research revealed that a significant portion of ethnic executives assume roles like chief technology officers (CTO) or chief operations officers (COO), but fewer reach the positions of chief executive officer (CEO) or chairperson. When I engaged with Sami to understand this phenomenon, he pointed out that this distinction might stem from the fact that roles like CEO and chairperson demand political skills and capabilities, areas where immigrants may need more proficiency in their new contexts. Immigrants often showcase their technical expertise and knowledge domains in adoptive societies, leading to promotions in those areas. However, a prevailing assumption is that immigrants might face challenges in roles requiring a profound understanding of the political landscape, a skill typically honed through lifelong socialization in specific circles.

CEO and chairperson positions inherently involve politics—corporate politics and social politics—demanding a deep understanding of networks, social backgrounds, and contexts to lead organizations effectively and garner support. Societal perceptions, including factors like religion or ethnicity, play a role, and society at large may not reflect an organization's tolerance of these factors.

While there is a global shift with individuals of immigrant backgrounds assuming high leadership positions, the question remains: How vital are political skills for leadership, and can immigrants develop these skills? If so, how can they learn to thrive in such environments through networking, involvement in political parties, or specific socialization? Leaders need to help immigrants build these types of networks.

Encouraging active participation in various community levels is essential, such as joining local religious institutions, engaging in local politics, volunteering, or socializing. Political organizations, in particular, play a significant role. Recent historical achievements—such as a person of Pakistani origin becoming the first minister for Scotland and the prime minister of the UK having an Indian background—showcase the importance of political affiliations in overcoming cultural obstacles and projecting oneself as a competent politician.

The challenge lies in the perception that immigrants, despite their competence, are not fully assimilated, reinforcing the notion that they are "not one of us." This becomes particularly pronounced when an immigrant retains an accent or has a distinctly different name. The persistent alienation experienced by immigrants makes it imperative for organizations to help immigrants build community and contribute to society beyond professional achievements.

The complex interplay of skills, societal integration, and perceptions poses a nuanced challenge for immigrants, highlighting the need for a holistic approach to address professional competence and the social and cultural dimensions of their identity in their adoptive societies.

Networking plays a significant role in career advancement and professional success. For immigrant leaders, networking is vital as it helps them overcome barriers and build connections in new environments. Through networking, immigrant leaders can meet professionals from various backgrounds, industries, and experience levels. These interactions enable them to gain insights, exchange ideas, and learn from others who have faced similar challenges or navigated the path to leadership.

Networking events, conferences, and industry-specific gatherings allow immigrant leaders to showcase their skills and expertise. Attending these events will enable them to learn about industry trends and best practices while offering opportunities to meet potential mentors, sponsors, and collaborators. By actively participating in networking activities, immigrant leaders can expand their professional circles, establish new relationships, and uncover hidden opportunities.

Community engagement is another essential aspect of nurturing immigrant leaders. Immigrant professionals bring diverse perspectives and experiences that can positively impact their communities. Engaging with community organizations, nonprofits, and volunteer initiatives allows immigrant leaders to give back and provides a platform to develop and showcase their leadership skills.

Community engagement allows collaboration with individuals from diverse backgrounds, fostering cross-cultural understanding and appreciation. However, building a solid network and engaging with the community requires effort and intentionality. Leaders can start by helping immigrants identify community organizations that align with their interests as a way to build their political capital.

Organizations can also play a role in facilitating networking and community engagement for immigrant leaders. They can organize internal networking events, leverage these digital platforms or online networking platforms, and offer avenues for immigrant leaders to feel connected and empowered. Additionally, encouraging immigrant leaders to engage with their communities within and outside the workplace can foster a sense of belonging, strengthen social capital, and provide avenues for leadership and community involvement.

Networking and community engagement are essential for cultivating immigrant leaders. These activities coupled with right-size leadership development programs, mentorship, and sponsorship programs provide the foundation for cultivating ImmiGRIT. But one last pivotal question now demands our attention. After an organization cultivates ImmiGRIT, how does it sustain it?

CHAPTER 11

SUSTAINING IMMIGRIT

Sustain /verb/ to cause or allow something to continue.

In the bustling halls of higher education across the US, a striking phenomenon is unfolding. A significant portion of enrolled students are of immigrant origin. Immigrant-origin students are a blend of first- and second-generation immigrants, each carrying a unique narrative of migration, adaptation, and aspiration. First-generation immigrants were born abroad and immigrated to the US to live. Second-generation immigrants are US-born individuals with at least one immigrant parent. These students represent not only the landscape of higher education but the future of the workforce. It is highly probable that a student entering the workforce today, freshly recruited from a US university, bears immigrant roots.

Within the vast expanse of higher education, immigrant-origin and international students make up one-third of the student body.[1] As of 2021, the count of immigrant-origin students stands impressively at 5.6 million, representing a formidable 31 percent of all higher education students nationwide.[2] Notably, over 80 percent of these students hail from diverse racial and ethnic backgrounds, infusing campuses with a vibrant spectrum of perspectives and experiences.[3] Moreover, this dynamic cohort has played a pivotal role in the growth of US higher education enrollments, spearheading an astonishing 80 percent of the increase between 2000 and 2021.[4]

While many organizations focus on monitoring and increasing their diverse, nonwhite hires—with one in three university students already hailing from diverse backgrounds—this, in theory, should not be a complex endeavor. However, organizations should give more attention to the central task of sustaining this diverse talent pool. Attaining immigrant leadership can only be realized when organizations effectively encourage talent, ensuring full engagement and contribution.

At the onset of value implementation initiatives, like increasing the representation of immigrant leaders, there's a tendency to quantify organizational diversity and rush into creating new programs. However, this approach may need to be revised. Merely creating programs without dedicated drivers and sponsors often leads to short-lived success. Instead, a more effective strategy involves integrating diversity into all organizational processes, fostering an environment where employees feel empowered to contribute as their authentic selves and seamlessly integrate into the corporate fabric.

Although immigrants undoubtedly require support, they also deserve protection from discrimination and bias. A supportive or protective infrastructure only addresses surface-level issues. The real challenge lies in sustaining healthy cultures conducive to immigrant leadership.

The question we must confront in this chapter is: How do we do that? We'll discuss the essential pillars for sustaining ImmiGRIT: fostering a sense of belonging, prioritizing well-being, and advocating for immigrant rights.

PILLAR 1: FOSTERING A SENSE OF BELONGING

Belonging is the cornerstone of human fulfillment, intricately woven into our most pressing modern dilemmas. Its absence leaves individuals adrift while its presence fosters growth and flourishing. Yet despite its profound impact, belonging often goes unnoticed due to its elusive nature.

I must confess my initial reaction to organizations appending the letter "B" for belonging to the well-established DEI acronym, thus forming DEIB, was skepticism. Belonging seemed like a hasty addition, needing more depth for genuine inclusivity. I questioned whether creating a sense of belonging in the workplace would inevitably lead to forced assimilation rather than organic integration.

However, my perspective shifted as I uncovered the facts. In the workplace, a staggering 64 percent of individuals don't feel like they belong, and nearly 20 percent lack a sense of belonging in any life setting.[5] These deficits in belonging can impose significant costs on both individuals and institutions. Workplaces that have cultivated a healthy sense of belonging are likely to see more employee creativity, better job performance (even among CEOs), increased organizational loyalty, higher retention rates among workers, and fewer employee health complaints and missed days at work.

Investing in belonging is more critical than ever in today's polarized, socially segregated, increasingly diverse world. Fortunately, there's a growing body of research on effective belonging interventions, with organizations and communities already piloting such efforts.[6] Understanding what works, what doesn't, and why will be essential for advancing the field as this work progresses.

As with everything, how an organization creates the sense of belonging matters. Many facets of an experience influence how one fits or could fit within an environment, but at the core is psychological safety. Over the past two decades, research in organizational psychology has highlighted the vital role of psychological safety for human resources and collaborative teams.[7] This concept gained widespread attention in the business world in 2015 when Google identified it as the foremost factor associated with high-performing teams.[8] Surprisingly, psychological safety proved more influential than several conventional predictors of team success, including the number of top performers, collective team intelligence, consensus-driven decision-making, overall workload or stress levels, and physical proximity of team members.

It became evident that when individuals feel empowered to share dissenting views, diverse perspectives, or unconventional ideas—actions facilitated by psychological safety—their teams demonstrate enhanced problem-solving capabilities, leading to quicker and more creative solutions. While psychological safety, essentially feeling secure enough to be vulnerable and take risks, has primarily been studied and applied in business contexts, its underlying mechanism holds relevance for any collaborative community, whether it's a family, friend group, or local community.

Understanding belonging is fundamental for leaders and stakeholders across various sectors who aim to sustain immigrant talent.

One effective mechanism for creating a psychologically safe space is establishing employee resource groups (ERGs) dedicated to immigrant experiences. These groups serve as sanctuaries within the organizational structure where individuals can share their stories, seek advice, and find understanding among peers who share similar journeys.

The inception of the Xerox National Black Employees Caucus in 1970 marked a pivotal moment in corporate history, establishing the first official employee resource group (ERG) in the US.[9] Designed as a platform for Black employees to advocate for inclusivity and reform within their company, it paved the way for a proliferation of ERGs nationwide. Today, an impressive 90 percent of Fortune 500 companies boast ERGs, showcasing their widespread adoption and recognition.[10]

ERGs have evolved into more structured entities with distinct governance frameworks, missions, and strategies in recent years. Many now play integral roles in advancing their company's diversity, equity, and inclusion (DEI) initiatives. Research by McKinsey & Company reveals that ERGs excel particularly in community building, surpassing other dimensions such as leadership engagement and career advancement.[11]

Eager to gauge the landscape of immigrant-centered ERGs, I polled my LinkedIn audience, which is comprised of nearly three thousand followers. Astonishingly, 86 percent of respondents reported a lack of an immigrant ERG within their organizations. The absence of an immigrant ERG is a missed opportunity not only for immigrant employees but also for employers. Collaborating with ERGs offers companies invaluable insights into employee needs and experiences, aiding in product development, process refinement, and talent identification. Moreover, fostering a culture of inclusivity through ERGs contributes to enhanced internal awareness and cohesion, ultimately bolstering employee retention.

At the same time, ERG members are indispensable organizational ambassadors amid shifting demographics, globalization, and the demand for personalized products. Their firsthand knowledge of diverse markets and consumer preferences equips companies with vital information for effective market penetration and product adaptation. For instance, an immigrant ERG may conduct focus groups to inform marketing strategies tailored to immigrant communities. Additionally, ERGs serve as conduits for establishing strategic partnerships with customers, clients, and suppliers, enhancing organizational visibility and fostering relationships in key markets.

Essentially, ERGs foster inclusivity and belonging within companies and are a strategic asset for navigating today's dynamic marketplace. Embracing the insights of ERG members is essential for companies striving to remain agile, responsive, and competitive in an increasingly diverse and interconnected world. If your organization does not have one yet, it needs one!

Here are a few tips to help create an immigrant ERG:

- Find a few employees who are passionate about connecting with and helping other immigrant employees to lead the group and engage others.
- Focus on networking and peer mentoring; neither costs anything and can be implemented with minimal training. These activities can help build employees' leadership skills.
- Connect to community organizations that can offer training and mentoring programs.

PILLAR 2: PRIORITIZE WELL-BEING

Employee stress levels have steadily climbed over the past decade, posing significant challenges for businesses worldwide. According to Gallup's 2022 Workplace report, a staggering 44 percent of employees reported experiencing high stress levels the previous day, marking the second consecutive year of record-breaking stress among workers.[12] This alarming trend shows a link between mental health and overall workplace performance, highlighting the urgent need for robust support systems within organizations.

A customer poll conducted by ComPsych, the world's largest provider of behavioral health and well-being services, reveals that 87 percent of employers identified mental health support as their top priority for employees.[13] This reflects a growing recognition of the importance of employee well-being in driving productivity, reducing absenteeism, improving work quality, and ensuring workplace safety. Additionally, nearly 100 percent of employees themselves cited mental health support as a top concern, underscoring the widespread need for adequate resources and interventions.[14]

Navigating the challenges of being an international student and immigrant adds another layer of complexity to the already demanding workplace environment. Although immigrants possess the resilience to confront these obstacles head-on, sometimes the burden becomes overwhelming. As an immigrant leader with experience spanning various professional domains, including corporate, private practice, and government, I'd be remiss to spotlight a critical yet often overlooked aspect of leadership discourse concerning immigrants—the mental toll of immigration policies.

The impact of immigration policies extends far beyond the professional realm, profoundly affecting the mental well-being of immigrants. Discrimination in the workplace has been linked to poor mental health outcomes and deteriorating self-reported health status. To cultivate a workplace environment for immigrants, organizations should prioritize creating a safe space where individuals feel empowered to discuss the emotional challenges posed by immigration policies openly. Doing this reduces the mental toll that immigration has on immigrants. The ever-evolving landscape of immigration regulations breeds fears, frustrations, and uncertainties.

Employment and working conditions are key determinants of health. Workplace discrimination is associated with poor mental health and worsening self-reported health status.[15] In the pursuit of an immigrant-inclusive workplace, it's paramount to establish a safe space where immigrants feel comfortable discussing the emotional toll of immigration policies.

This space transcends the confines of typical workplace dialogue, delving deep into the profound fears, frustrations, and uncertainties inherent in navigating the constantly shifting landscape of immigration regulations. Conversations surrounding issues such as border walls, deportation, and the separation of immigrant children carry profound significance for the mental well-being of immigrant employees, just as discussions about the Black Lives Matter Movement impact the mental health of Black employees.

Yet we see a concerning tendency for these discussions to pit one issue against the other, exacerbating the stress and sense of isolation experienced by individuals who straddle multiple identities and face intersecting challenges. As a Black immigrant, I find myself equally affected by both sets of issues, yet the lack of acknowledgment and dialogue surrounding them, or the emphasis on one without the other, only serves to compound the emotional burden. Organizations must recognize the interconnectedness of these issues and foster an inclusive environment where all employees feel heard, supported, and valued.

In my own experience, I have found solace in environments that welcomed and actively encouraged open conversations about the emotional impact of immigration policies. This therapeutic approach fosters community and support, acknowledging immigrants' unique challenges.

Research suggests that immigrants are less likely than their local-born counterparts to seek out or be referred to mental health services, even when they experience comparable levels of distress.[16] This reflects both structural and cultural barriers, including the lack of mobility or ability to take time away from work, lack of linguistically accessible services, a desire to deal with problems on their own, the concern that practitioners will not understand their problems because of cultural or linguistic differences, and fear of stigmatization.

Beyond the mental toll, immigration policies carry a multifaceted impact that extends far beyond the professional realm. The intricate dance of paperwork, visa regulations, and uncertain residency statuses intertwines with personal lives. In my journey, I've grappled with the intricacies of legal requirements and experienced firsthand knowledge of how uncertainty in immigration policies impacts individuals and their families.

EMPLOYEE ASSISTANCE PROGRAMS

Understanding the weight of these challenges, organizations committed to supporting immigrants must go beyond rhetoric. They must actively familiarize their immigrant workforce with resources catering to their overall well-being. One effective mechanism is using the employee assistant program (EAP) to offer programs beneficial to immigrants. Establishing an immigration program for your company can feel like a daunting process. Immigration is a complicated subject, and you'll need to answer several questions: Which visas and green cards should your company support? What are the associated costs? What are the benefits, and most importantly, where do you start?

EAPs are intervention-style systems that offer employees benefits and promote a better work-life balance. They can provide counselors and other resources to employees experiencing personal challenges impacting work productivity. EAPs can also step in and help employees through workplace conflicts.

EAPs help employees address a myriad of issues:

- marital problems
- substance abuse
- mental disorders or imbalances
- financial struggles
- family issues
- emotional problems

In addition to these traditional areas of support, employers must start including immigration services in the scope of EAP offerings. Many EAPs even help employees with referrals, offering solutions for marital counseling, adoption assistance, childcare, elderly care services, and health and wellness programs. While workplaces set up EAPs, the specific services provided to individuals remain confidential.

When employees grapple with mental health and stress-related issues, it not only affects their well-being but also impacts their job performance, ultimately influencing business outcomes. Recognizing this, investing in well-designed EAPs goes beyond addressing immediate concerns and contributes to fostering a workplace culture that prioritizes the holistic well-being of employees, thereby sustaining talent.

Appropriately tailored with immigrants in mind, EAPs can serve as vital resources in providing comprehensive support to immigrant employees. When thoughtfully crafted, these programs offer confidential counseling, legal advice, and referral services tailored to address immigrant workers' unique challenges. For instance, a robust EAP may include legal professionals proficient in immigration policies, delivering personalized guidance to employees navigating the complexities of visa regulations. Such a personal approach acknowledges the distinct hurdles immigrants encounter and ensures they receive the specialized support needed to thrive in the workplace.

American Express is a noteworthy example of comprehensive support for employee well-being through a hybrid EAP approach to support physical and mental health needs.[17] Through the expansion of its EAP and the introduction of on-site professionals for face-to-face counseling sessions, the company witnessed a remarkable doubling in utilization rates.

In its concerted efforts to destigmatize mental health conditions, American Express has embarked on comprehensive communication, education, and behavior change initiatives under the "Healthy Minds" banner. These endeavors include impactful campaigns like "I Will Listen," featuring renowned actress Glenn Close, and the "Time to Talk" initiative, which encourages open dialogues about mental health among employees.[18]

The company has also integrated evidence-based practices and cultural considerations into its behavior change programs and resources, effectively catering to the needs of marginalized communities, including immigrants who may face unique challenges and stigmas in seeking help. This inclusive approach encompasses online applications teaching cognitive behavior therapy skills, webinars in multiple time zones, and a meditation program accessible via telephone. [19]

Leadership support has been pivotal in driving American Express's employee well-being initiatives, with senior leaders actively engaging in wellness efforts. Through frequent blogs for managers, regular participation in leadership meetings, and visible involvement in wellness initiatives, company leaders have demonstrated a tangible commitment to promoting employee well-being and fostering a culture of openness around mental health discussions. This proactive stance not only destigmatizes mental health but exemplifies how companies can support employees' holistic health and wellness, which results in sustaining talent.[20]

Here are some tips to create practical immigrant-informed EAPs:

SET UP AN EAP COMMITTEE. Create a committee to review your options. EAP committees could include members of human resources (HR), people management, leadership, or a mix of employees, including immigrants from different departments. Smaller companies should keep committees relatively lean while larger companies might want all HR and leadership involved.

DETERMINE A SUITABLE EAP MODEL FOR YOUR ORGANIZATION. Discuss the right EAP delivery model for your company. Determine if a fixed-fee or contract EAP system makes the most sense. Or if your company is large enough and can benefit from on-site services, consider hiring a professional or team to join your business.

DEVELOP AN EAP POLICY. An effective policy articulates the program's purpose, objectives, and scope, emphasizing confidentiality and accessibility while delineating services encompassing counseling, crisis intervention, and referral assistance. It ensures coverage clarity, integration with other workplace initiatives, and avenues for promotion and awareness to encourage employee utilization.

CONTINUOUSLY REVIEW YOUR EAP'S PROGRESS. To get the most out of your EAP, you'll want to consistently check on how often employees are taking advantage of these services, regularly communicate any new services, and make sure talent management alerts potential new employees of the benefits your company's EAP can provide.

PILLAR 3: ADVOCACY

Did you know 87 percent of Americans will purchase a product because a company advocated for an issue they cared about, and 76 percent will refuse to do business with a company with disliked policies?[21] Speaking out on social issues is essential for today's companies to remain competitive and sustain talent.

The business landscape is experiencing a transformation marked by a widespread embrace of corporate social responsibility (CSR) among established corporations and burgeoning start-ups. Notably, the integration of CSR into business models has become ubiquitous, with a staggering 90 percent of companies listed on the S&P 500 index releasing CSR reports in 2019, a stark increase from just 20 percent in 2011, as Harvard Business School Online reported.[22] Today, CSR efforts are motivated by customer feedback (19 percent), government mandates (16 percent), and public perception (15 percent).[23]

While profitability remains the primary objective for a business, the mounting pressure from consumers and employees to demonstrate tangible contributions to societal betterment is driving the rise of CSR programs. Consequently, CSR initiatives are evolving from mere ethical considerations at the executive level to foundational pillars of organizational culture and retaining talent, fostering collaboration between leaders and staff to drive positive change beyond corporate confines. When executed correctly, CSR programs balance purpose, product, and profit to create shared value for all stakeholders—customers, investors, and society.

At the moment, America's most polarizing social issues—immigration and guns—make the top of the list. Companies are increasingly finding it necessary to identify and implement workable, although not perfect, solutions. Sometimes, the course of action directly responds to public stakeholder pressure. Other times, companies quietly address issues as they arise for employees. For instance, corporate leaders know that anti-immigrant sentiment can chill innovation and entrepreneurship, which is hardly a circumstance they welcome. Therefore, many companies are supporting their employees' citizenship journeys. For those employees with friends and families entangled in immigration challenges, employers often support the process or help their affected associates cope.

For example, in 2017, leaders of major corporations took a stand against President Donald Trump's temporary immigration ban.[24] Executives at technology companies, which employ many immigrants, were some of the first to speak out, showcasing a pivotal moment in corporate advocacy for immigration. Heads of Apple, Ford, and

Goldman Sachs publicly declared their opposition to the executive order, which restricted immigrants from seven Muslim-majority nations from entering the US. In solidarity, Google pledged financial support to organizations aiding immigrants while companies like Starbucks committed to hiring refugees and assisting affected employees. In the face of such contentious policies, corporate leaders assert their values and leverage their influence to champion inclusivity and support for marginalized communities. These actions invoke loyalty and sustain talent.

As companies are compelled to take a public stance on controversial issues, they find some middle ground in protecting the bottom line while appeasing consumers and stakeholders. Even if a company doesn't take a hardline position that answers all the activist demands (such as open borders), it is figuring out how to drive change while addressing lost revenue and other risks. No company has ever gone out of business by putting its customers and employees first.

No company has ever gone out of business by putting its customers and employees first.

Organizations should visibly commit to advocating fair and equitable opportunities for advancement and addressing unconscious bias to create an environment that sustains immigrant leaders. Organizations should actively seek out and amplify the voices of immigrant leaders and provide platforms for sharing their stories and experiences.

Advocacy plays a key role in raising awareness about the challenges faced by immigrant leaders and advocating for their rights and equal treatment. Advocacy efforts can include lobbying for policy changes, engaging in public discourse, and partnering with community organizations to promote inclusivity. By highlighting immigrant leaders' values, advocacy can help change perceptions and overcome biases that may hinder their progress.

Fostering a sense of belonging, prioritizing well-being, and advocating for immigrant rights are the essential pillars for sustaining ImmiGRIT, and within these pillars, I have provided some effective strategies.

* * *

Before I turn to my conclusion, we must recognize that the pillars for sustaining ImmiGRIT rests on the foundation of DEI. Diversity and inclusion are not just buzzwords; they hold immense power to transform organizations and societies.

Diversity and inclusion are beneficial not only within organizations but also within societies. As communities become more diverse, it is important to have leaders who understand and appreciate these diversities. Immigrant leaders are often well-equipped to build bridges between cultural groups, fostering social cohesion and harmony. In addition, diversity and inclusion promote fairness and equity. By embracing immigrant leaders, organizations demonstrate their commitment to equal opportunities for all.

The power of diversity and inclusion cannot be overstated. Immigrant leaders may bring their perspectives, experiences, and talents that fuel innovation, foster collaboration, and drive success, but organizations must embrace diversity first in order to unlock the fullest potential immigrant leadership to drive organization success, serve their clients and customers, and make their communities better.

PARTING WORDS

A Nobel Prize-winning physicist, Dennis Gabor, once said, "The future cannot be predicted, but futures can be invented."[1] The future will require leaders who are global citizens, able to work in a multicultural environment, value talent, and embrace transformation. The future needs workplaces that value ImmiGRIT.

The era of immigrant leadership is upon us. Companies must tap into the vast talent pool that immigrants represent to thrive in a rapidly changing world. They must recognize and appreciate the unique perspectives, skills, and experiences immigrant leaders offer. They must have leadership that reflects their workforce and the communities they serve. By doing so, they can unlock a new era of growth and profitability.

As I conclude this book, I think about the story of a global messaging platform that I use multiple times daily. I am among the more than 2.24 billion people who use WhatsApp monthly.[2] This makes WhatsApp one of the world's most popular mobile messaging applications. In the fast-paced landscape of digital communication, WhatsApp is a technological success. Since its humble beginnings in

2009, this instant messaging giant, founded by Jan Koum, a Ukrainian immigrant, has revolutionized how we connect and has achieved a staggering feat: handling a daily load of fifty billion messages with a remarkably lean team.

In his compelling TED Talk "How Your Company Can Gain a Global Talent Advantage," Johann Daniel Harnoss, a partner and associate director at Boston Consulting Group (BCG) leading the global program on Innovation without Borders, shares an illuminating conversation that ties together everything I have discussed in this book. He recounts his discussion with one of the early engineers at WhatsApp, revealing the pivotal role that immigrants had in the app's development. He shares, "WhatsApp was developed by a global team that resembled a mini United Nations."[3] Despite the fact WhatsApp was founded in the US, it was intentionally designed not just for the average US college student but with a truly global audience in mind.

To do this, they built a team led by an immigrant software developer. However, throughout the development journey, the immigrant leader posed questions to the team: Would the app function effectively in remote areas of Africa and Asia? Could it serve refugees communicating with their families from boats? These considerations led to WhatsApp becoming a product built in the US but tailored for the world through actual perspectives of immigrants, illustrating the power of immigrant-inclusive diversity in innovation.

WhatsApp is not just an outlier. Other groundbreaking products like Pfizer-BioNTech vaccines, Google Search, YouTube, and the iPhone were also developed collaboratively by immigrant and local teams. Leading companies recognize the value of hiring immigrants for their insights and unique perspectives. They now need to go one step further—advance them to executive leadership.

Companies struggle to follow the lead of WhatsApp and others, so Johann and his team at BCG dug deeper. They interviewed eight hundred and fifty executives in a recent BCG survey, finding that 95 percent said they see the value in hiring immigrants.[4] However, only 5 percent stated they were already doing it strategically and getting the results.[5] With 280 million international migrants worldwide and a potential 750 million more willing to relocate globally, migration presents a unique opportunity for strategic advantage, benefiting both companies and nations alike.[6] To effect change, senior executives must prioritize hiring initiatives and immigrant leadership.

I am not naive to the fact that immigration has become a central issue in contemporary politics. Its significance, however, is often misunderstood. The primary challenge isn't visa issues; most countries offer straightforward paths to work for qualified individuals. Instead, the problem lies within the business realm and organizational culture. In reality, migration is linked to broader economic transformations rather than migration itself. The rise of anti-immigrant sentiment is fueled by the alienation and economic insecurity experienced by specific segments of society, particularly those affected by factors such as automation, globalization, and financial market instability.

Despite the rise of technology and artificial intelligence (AI), a strong and emerging case says the future of work will involve humans. The evidence suggests humans are indispensable. Human talent—not capital, technology, or anything else—is the key factor linking innovation, competitiveness, and growth in the twenty-first century.

The most challenging task for leaders now and in the future is maximizing the potential of their workforce.

The most challenging task for leaders now and in the future is maximizing the potential of their workforce. Leaders must prepare to navigate the inevitable changes, including the increasing impact of migration. Understanding employees' diverse backgrounds is essential for effective leadership, as it directly influences their work dynamics. Even for companies with primarily local operations, having clients and customers from immigrant backgrounds underscores the importance of cultural awareness and inclusivity in delivering products and services.

As we navigate an ever-evolving landscape shaped by technological advancements, shifting demographics, the rise of the global middle class, and environmental factors like climate change, leaders must guide their teams through these changes. According to a survey conducted by the World Economic Forum among chief human resources officers, social skills such as adaptability, resilience, and resourcefulness are poised to become more valuable across industries.[7] Prioritizing investment in these social skills is the key to successfully managing disruptions to the labor market in the long term.

Our exploration into *ImmiGRIT* has illuminated the remarkable potential inherent in immigrant talent and its profound impact on organizational culture. Improved culture leads to improved profits. We have explored the experiences, perspectives, and strengths embodied within ImmiGRIT. We know what immigrants bring to the table. We have witnessed firsthand how their contributions can reshape organizations, drive innovation, increase profitability, and foster an inclusive environment that cultivates success and prosperity for all.

Research into the future of work almost always ignores another vital force shaping the US labor market—immigration. Immigrant-origin workers—immigrants and their US-born children—have been the main drivers of US workforce growth in recent years. They were responsible for 83 percent of labor force growth between 2010 and 2018, at which point they comprised 28 percent of all US workers.[8] Projections suggest that through 2035, all growth in the working-age population will come from immigrant-origin adults.[9]

By the year 2030, a staggering global shortfall of human talent is projected to exceed eighty-five million individuals, a figure roughly equivalent to the entire population of Germany.[10] If left unaddressed, this talent deficit could lead to approximately $8.5 trillion in missed revenues annually. Migration is expected to be critical in mitigating this shortfall, with talent crossing borders and searching for opportunities to fill critical roles.

Consequently, by 2035, immigrants will represent more than 20 percent of working-age adults in the US workforce. Immigrants are vital to the US labor market, but our workplaces must fully leverage the assets of our growing immigrant workforce.[11] Immigrant leadership is the next step in realizing the economic potential for American employers and communities.

With automation rising, future jobs will mainly be high- or middle-skilled. Future jobs are concentrated in health care, education, management, and social service occupations. The most common industries for immigrants in the US to work in are educational and health services, which the Census Bureau groups together, and the professional and business services industries. These are also the largest industries overall in the US. More immigrant workers were in every industry tracked by the Census Bureau in 2022 compared to 2010.[12] The share of immigrant workers increased by more than three percentage points from 2010 to 2022.[13]

It's time to embrace immigrant leadership and weave it into the very fabric of our organizations. It's time to build cultures that celebrate diversity, empower all employees, and drive innovation. It's time for immigrant leadership. This is a call to action for companies to rise above the ordinary and seize the opportunity to transform their company cultures. Let us remember that the future of work lies not in scapegoating immigrants but in addressing the structural leadership inequalities that underpin our societies and inhibit profits.

We need more people in leadership with the lived experiences of immigrants—those who feel the weight of it and understand the unrelenting mental ticker that rolls through the minds of those facilitating the lives of their families. These leaders, who see and understand it themselves, are better positioned to support their teams.

This is the moment to rethink leadership. The work is just beginning. May *ImmiGRIT* catalyze dialogue, reflection, and action—a blueprint for building a more equitable leadership bench in corporations worldwide for generations to come.

Let's lead differently!

ACKNOWLEDGMENTS

"If you want to go fast, go alone.
If you want to go far, go together."

—AFRICAN PROVERB

Writing a book has never been a dream of mine. So when that graduating international student praised my commencement speech, telling me, "You should write a book," I laughed it off initially.

Then, I said the prayer I say before I take on a project I have no idea how to begin, a prayer I learned from *New York Times* bestselling author Luvvie Ajayi Jones: "May my people find me."

And you all did!

Writing this book, all while working a full-time job as a lawyer, parenting two young active children, and governing a city, can only happen with the support of a village.

I want to start by thanking my sisters: Debbie, Nti, Inyene, Ofonime, and my parents: Comfort and Allen. Our family group chat is my constant source of strength. Your ability to remain unfazed by any idea I drop in there, bolstered by your automatic support of my dreams, is the rarest gift of all. It is heartwarming to feel the never-ending support of family.

To my children, Aubrey and Zachary... *My A to Z,* thank you for holding steady. I felt so supported by both of you for your simple questions like: "How is the writing going, Mommy?" and, "We can do it ourselves if you need to get back to writing." I hope I have modeled for you how to work toward your goals.

Brian and Gab, thank you for envisioning Book Camp. Being part of that inaugural cohort jumpstarted the writing of this book. Thank you to all the cohort members for keeping me inspired and motivated.

My deepest gratitude goes to the immigrants, leaders, researchers, and thought leaders who committed their time and contributed their expertise to this book. Your interviews and insights brought the concepts shared in this book into focus. Thank you for trusting me with your stories.

To everyone who has played a role in my leadership journey—whether as former colleagues, classmates, mentors, or sponsors—know this book is a combination and cumulation of many lessons I've learned from you along the way. I wouldn't be the leader I am without you. To Joey Neadeau, my first boss, you ignited my ImmiGRIT and set the standard. Thank you.

To Eugina Jordan, thank you for penning the foreword to this book. You epitomize ImmiGRIT.

To my remarkable Manuscripts LLC revisions editor, Frances Chiu: Thank you for believing in this project as much as I did. Your ability to be critical and graceful with your feedback and get in the trenches to ensure my prose conveyed what I meant was such a gift.

To my beta readers: Nicole Makeda, Julie Collins, Chris Catania, Sadie Palmisano, Kimberly Hartsfield, Christol Cook, Brian Trotier, Jennifer Landgren, Medha Kapil, and Carrie Narcelles, thank you for providing feedback on early drafts. You have made this book *so* much better. Extra special thanks to my friend Sherrie Gilbert, owner of Prep & Prose LLC, for the editing and providing invaluable feedback on my entire manuscript.

To my friends who offered endless humor, provided unintended therapy, and refilled my cup when I ran low on morale: thank you, Medha Kapil (my MVP), Kimberly Hartsfield, Zainab Hartford, Mary Lehnaetz, Abiola Afolayan, Emmanuel Olawale, Tina Jones, Sandra Brogdon, Bose Okonrende, my Renegade Fam and my beloved friends in the Golden Scoots group chat, the funniest group chat on the planet!

To all those who contributed to my book campaign, your generosity has made this book possible: Thank you from the bottom of my heart, with extra special thanks to Medha Kapil, Michael Gordon, and the Women of Taft-Columbus for not sparing any change.

To Manuscripts LLC, thank you for making me an author!

Finally, to you, the reader, thank you for investing your time in this book and allowing me the privilege to share my thoughts.

NOTES

INTRODUCTION

1. Sharon Gillenwater, "Today's Immigrant CEOs: Bringing a Global Sensibility to American Business," *The 360 Blog (blog)*, *Salesforce*, November 3, 2020, https://www.salesforce.com/blog/immigrant-ceos-global-sensibility-business-blog.

2. United Nations, n.d., "The Number of International Migrants Reaches 272 Million, Continuing an Upward Trend in All World Regions, Says UN," *United Nations*, accessed February 21, 2024, https://www.un.org/uk/desa/number-international-migrants-reaches-272-million-continuing-upward-trend-all.

3. Abby Budiman, "Key Findings About US Immigrants," *Immigration & Migration* (blog), *Pew Research Center,* August 20, 2020, https://www.pewresearch.org/short-reads/2020/08/20/key-findings-about-u-s-immigrants.

4. Richie Zweigenhaft, "Fortune 500 CEOs, 2000–2020: Still Male, Still White," *Special Feature* (blog), *The Society Pages*, October 28, 2020, https://thesocietypages.org/specials/fortune-500-ceos-2000-2020-still-male-still-white/.

5. Katy Smith, "Announcing Columbus CEO'S Future 50 Class of 2022 of Visionaries, Leaders, Doers," *News* (blog), *Columbus Urban League*, October 29, 2021, https://www.cul.

org/announcing-columbus-ceos-future-50-class-of-2022-of-visionaries-leaders-doers.

CHAPTER 1. FROM IMMIGRANT TO LEADER

1. History.com Editors, "John Rolfe," *Exploration* (blog), *History*, December 16, 2009, https://www.history.com/topics/exploration/john-rolfe.

2. Unzipped Staff, "The History of Denim," *Unzipped* (blog), *Levi Strauss & Co*, July 3, 2019, https://www.levistrauss.com/2019/07/04/the-history-of-denim.

3. The Immigrant Learning Center, "Sergey Brin," *Hall of Fame* (blog), *The Immigrant Learning Center*, https://www.ilctr.org/entrepreneur-hof/sergey-brin.

4. Joanne Chen, "American Dreamers: Zoom Founder Eric Yuan on Making His Mark in Silicon Valley," *Venture Capital* (blog), *Forbes*, July 11, 2022, https://www.forbes.com/sites/joannechen/2022/07/11/american-dreamers-zoom-founder-eric-yuan-on-making-his-mark-in-silicon-valley.

5. Juliana Kaplan, "Meet Moderna's Cofounder and Chairman, Whose Coronavirus Vaccine Is Now Approved on Both Sides of the Atlantic. He Loves Basketball and Dolly Parton," *Healthcare* (blog), *Business Insider*, January 6, 2021, https://www.businessinsider.com/meet-noubar-afeyan-chairman-cofounder-of-moderna-coronavirus-vaccine-fda-2020-12.

6. Levi Strauss & Co, "Levi Strauss & Co Reports Fourth-Quarter and Fiscal Year 2022 Financial Results," *Financial News* (blog), *Levi Strauss & Co*, https://bit.ly/49Iozc1.

7. Gennaro Cuofano, "Google Revenue Breakdown," *Business* (blog), *FourWeekMBA*, February 5, 2024, https://fourweekmba.com/google-revenue-breakdown.

8. Anayat Durrani, "International Student Numbers in US Show Fastest Growth in 40 Years," *Best Global Universities* (blog), *US News & World Report*, November 28, 2023, https://www.

usnews.com/education/best-global-universities/articles/
international-student-numbers-in-u-s-show-fastest-growth-
in-40-years.

9. USCIS (US Citizenship and Immigration Services), "H-1B Electronic Registration Process," *Temporary Workers* (blog), *USCIS*, February 14, 2024, https://www.uscis.gov/working-in-the-united-states/temporary-workers/h-1b-specialty-occupations-and-fashion-models/h-1b-electronic-registration-process.

CHAPTER 2. THE SHIFTING LANDSCAPE OF IMMIGRATION

1. Nicole Ward and Jeanne Batalova, "Frequently Requested Statistics on Immigrants and Immigration in the United States," *Migration Information Source* (blog), *Migration Policy Institute*, March 14, 2023, https://www.migrationpolicy.org/article/frequently-requested-statistics-immigrants-and-immigration-united-states.

2. Christopher Klein, "Why Did the Pilgrims Come to America?" *Colonial America* (blog), *History,* November 13, 2020, https://www.history.com/news/why-pilgrims-came-to-america-mayflower.

3. History.com Editors, "US Immigration Before 1965," *Immigration* (blog), *History*, September 10, 2021, https://www.history.com/topics/immigration/u-s-immigration-before-1965.

4. Ibid.

5. James Truslow Adams, *The Epic of America* (Boston, MA: Little, Brown, and Company, 1931, 214–215.

6. History.com Editors, "US Immigration before 1965," *Immigration* (blog), *History*, September 10, 2021, https://www.history.com/topics/immigration/u-s-immigration-before-1965.

7. Ibid.

8. History.Com Editors, "US Immigration Before 1965," *Immigration* (blog), *History*, September 10, 2021, https://www.history.com/topics/immigration/u-s-immigration-before-1965.

9. Ibid.

10 History.com Editors, "US Immigration Timeline," *Immigration* (blog), *History*, updated August 23, 2022, https://www.history.com/topics/immigration/immigration-united-states-timeline.

11. Ibid.

12. History.com Editors, "US Immigration Timeline," *Immigration* (blog), *History*, updated August 23, 2022, https://www.history.com/topics/immigration/immigration-united-states-timeline.

13. Ibid.

14. History.com Editors, "US Immigration Timeline," *Immigration* (blog), *History*, updated August 23, 2022, https://www.history.com/topics/immigration/immigration-united-states-timeline.

15. Ibid.

16. History.com Editors, "US Immigration Timeline," *Immigration* (blog), *History*, updated August 23, 2022, https://www.history.com/topics/immigration/immigration-united-states-timeline.

17. Ibid.

18. Re-Imagining Migration, "President Johnson and the 1965 Immigration Action," *Re-Imagining Migration* (blog), June 18, 2019, https://reimaginingmigration.org/president-johnson-and-the-1965-immigration-action.

19. Abby Budiman, "Key Findings About US Immigrants," *Immigration & Migration* (blog), *Pew Research Center*, August 20, 2020, https://www.pewresearch.org/short-reads/2020/08/20/key-findings-about-u-s-immigrants.

20. Ibid.

21. Ran Abramitzky and Leah Boustan, *Streets of Gold: America's Untold Story of Immigrant Success* (New York: PublicAffairs, 2022).

CHAPTER 3. IMMIGRATION IS SHAPING US

1. Chimamanda Ngozi Adichie, "The Danger of a Single Story," July 2009, TED video and transcript, 00:18:33, https://www.ted.com/talks/chimamanda_ngozi_adichie_the_danger_of_a_single_story/transcript.

2. William Frey, "New Census Estimates Show a Tepid Rise in US Population Growth, Buoyed by Immigration," *Research* (blog), *Brookings*, January 24, 2023, https://www.brookings.edu/articles/new-census-estimates-show-a-tepid-rise-in-u-s-population-growth-buoyed-by-immigration.

3. Luke Rogers, "COVID-19, Declining Birth Rates and International Migration Resulted in Historically Small Population Gains," *America Counts: Stories* (blog), United States Census Bureau, December 21, 2021, https://www.census.gov/library/stories/2021/12/us-population-grew-in-2021-slowest-rate-since-founding-of-the-nation.html.

4. US Census Bureau, "Hispanic Heritage Month: 2023," *Facts for Features* (blog), *United States Census Bureau*, August 17, 2023, https://www.census.gov/newsroom/facts-for-features/2023/hispanic-heritage-month.html.

5. Jonathan Vespa, David M. Armstrong, and Lauren Medina, "Demographic Turning Points for the United States: Population Projections for 2020 to 2060," *Publications* (blog) *United States Census Bureau*, February 2020, https://www.census.gov/library/publications/2020/demo/p25-1144.html.

6. Ibid.

7. Siri Roland Xavier, Donna Kelley, Jacqui Kew, Mike Herrington, and Arne Vorderwülbecke, *GEM 2012 Global Report* (London: Global Entrepreneurship Monitor), https://www.gemconsortium.org/report/gem-2012-global-report.

8. Shai Bernstein, Rebecca Diamond, Abhisit Jiranaphawiboon, Timothy McQuade, and Beatriz Pousada, "The Contribution of High-Skilled Immigrants to Innovation in the United States," NBER (National Bureau of Economic Research) Working Paper 30797, https://doi.org/10.3386/w30797.

9. Ibid.

10. Peter Vandor and Nikolaus Franke, "Why Are Immigrants More Entrepreneurial?" *Entrepreneurs and Founders* (blog), *Harvard Business Review,* August 31, 2021, https://hbr.org/2016/10/why-are-immigrants-more-entrepreneurial.

11. Andy Semotiuk, "US H-1B Visa Holders Targeted by Canada's New Immigration Program," *Policy* (blog), *Forbes,* June 28, 2023, https://www.forbes.com/sites/andyjsemotiuk/2023/06/28/us-h1-b-visa-holders-targeted-by-canadas-new-immigration-program/?sh=5d89485a59b5.

12. Hal Matthews, "You Should Know About the UK High Potential Individual Visa (HPI)," *Career Hub* (blog), *Duke University*, August 15, 2023, https://careerhub.students.duke.edu/blog/2023/08/21/you-should-know-about-the-uk-high-potential-individual-visa-hpi.

13. Alex Seitz-Wald, "Actually, Salsa Dethroned Ketchup 20 Years Ago," *US* (blog), *The Atlantic*, October 17, 2013, https://www.theatlantic.com/national/archive/2013/10/actually-salsa-dethroned-ketchup-20-years-ago/309844.

CHAPTER 4. UNVEILING IMMIGRANTS IN DIVERSITY DISCOURSE

1. Kimberle Crenshaw, "Demarginalizing the Intersection of Race and Sex: A Black Feminist Critique of Antidiscrimination Doctrine, Feminist Theory and Antiracist Politics," *University of Chicago Legal Forum* 1989, no. 1 (1989): 139–167, https://chicagounbound.uchicago.edu/cgi/viewcontent.cgi?article=1052&context=uclf.

2. Alex Ross, "Language Diversity: Learnings on Inclusivity and Accessibility," *Talk to Loop* (blog), *Loop*, January 21,

2024, https://talktoloop.org/blog-posts/language-diversity-learnings-on-inclusivity-and-accessibility.

3. Kevin Turausky, "The Jante Law and Racism: A Study on the Effects of Immigration on Swedish National Identity," (master's thesis, University of Massachusetts Amherst, 2014), https://scholarworks.umass.edu/theses/551.

4. Milan Hrabovský, "Etymology of the Word 'Race' and the Issue of the Concept of 'Race,'" self-published academic paper, 10, https://www.researchgate.net/publication/349426899_Etymology_of_the_Word_Race_and_the_Issue_of_the_Concept_of_Race.

5. Huw Beverley-Smith, Charlotte Marshall, and Elise Lanteri, "The Legalities of Collecting Workers' Diversity Data," *PM People Management* (blog), *CIPD*, March 3, 2022, https://www.peoplemanagement.co.uk/article/1751686/legalities-collecting-workers-diversity-data.

CHAPTER 5. UNCONSCIOUS BIASES IMPACTING IMMIGRANTS

1. Tsedal Neeley, "Global Business Speaks English," *Business Communication* (blog), *Harvard Business Review,* May, 2012, https://hbr.org/2012/05/global-business-speaks-english.

2. Paul Stevens, "Viewpoint: The Silencing of ESL Speakers," *News* (blog), *SHRM*, August 6, 2019, https://www.shrm.org/topics-tools/news/inclusion-equity-diversity/viewpoint-silencing-esl-speakers.

3. Ibid.

4. Rosina Lippi-Green, *English with an Accent: Language, Ideology, and Discrimination in the United States* (London: Routledge, 1997).

5. UNESCO, "Why Mother Language-Based Education Is Essential," *UNESCO*, updated April 20, 2023, https://www.unesco.org/en/articles/why-mother-language-based-education-essential.

6. Rosina Lippi-Green, *English with an Accent: Language, Ideology, and Discrimination in the United States* (London: Routledge, 1997), 88.

7. Renée K. Gadoua, "Nonnative English Speakers' Attitudes Towards Polish-Accented English," *Theoria Et Historia Scientiarum* 17 (January 2021): 77–94, https://doi.org/10.12775/ths.2020.003.

8. Jason Richwine, "Accent Discrimination: Invisible Source of Social Bias" *STEM (blog)* October 25, 2018, https://news.syr.edu/blog/2018/10/25/accent-discrimination-invisible-source-of-social-bias.

9. Cassie Arnita, "Barriers to Career Advancement among Skilled Immigrants in the US," *Issue Briefs* (blog), *Ballard Brief,* December, 2022, https://ballardbrief.byu.edu/issue-briefs/barriers-to-career-advancement-among-skilled-immigrants-in-the-us.

10. Lean In "The State of Black Women in Corporate America," *Workplace* (San Francisco, CA: Lean In, 2020), https://leanin.org/research/state-of-black-women-in-corporate-america/section-1-representation.

CHAPTER 6. ABSENCE OF IMMIGRANT LEADERSHIP

1. Abby Budiman, "Key Findings About US Immigrants," *Immigration & Migration* (blog), *Pew Research Center,* August 20, 2020, https://www.pewresearch.org/short-reads/2020/08/20/key-findings-about-u-s-immigrants.

2. Sharon Gillenwater, "Today's Immigrant CEOs: Bringing a Global Sensibility to American Business," *C-Suite* (blog), *Salesforce,* June 16, 2017, https://www.salesforce.com/blog/immigrant-ceos-global-sensibility-business-blog.

3. Sami Mahroum and Rashid Ansari, "What the Data Tells Us About Immigrant Executives in the US," *Consumer Behavior* (blog), *Harvard Business Review,* August 31, 2021, https://

hbr.org/2017/11/what-the-data-tells-us-about-immigrant-executives-in-the-u-s.

4. Anneke Jong, "You Can't Be What You Can't See: How to Get More Women in Tech," *Exploring Careers* (blog), *The Muse*, June 19, 2020, https://www.themuse.com/advice/you-cant-be-what-you-cant-see-how-to-get-more-women-in-tech.

5. Claudia Deutsch, "A Woman to Be Chief at PepsiCo," *Business* (blog), *New York Times*, August 15, 2006, https://www.nytimes.com/2006/08/15/business/15pepsi.html.

6. Arbora Johnson, "Indra Nooyi," *National Women's History Museum*, 2022, https://www.womenshistory.org/education-resources/biographies/indra-nooyi.

7. "Giants—Indra Nooyi—PepsiCo," *Giants* (blog), *Profit Magazine*, September 2020, https://profitmagazin.com/editions/number_136.1394.html.

8. Adi Ignatius, "Indra Nooyi, Former CEO of PepsiCo, on Nurturing Talent in Turbulent Times," *Business and Society* (blog), *Harvard Business Review*, November 5, 2021, https://hbr.org/2021/11/indra-nooyi-former-ceo-of-pepsico-on-nurturing-talent-in-turbulent-times.

9. Raju Narisetti and Indra Nooyi, "Author Talks: Indra Nooyi on Leadership, Life, and Crafting a Better Future," *Featured Insights* (blog), *McKinsey & Company*, October 8, 2021, https://www.mckinsey.com/featured-insights/mckinsey-on-books/author-talks-indra-nooyi-on-leadership-life-and-crafting-a-better-future.

10. Ibid.

11. Raju Narisetti and Indra Nooyi, "Author Talks: Indra Nooyi on Leadership, Life, and Crafting a Better Future," *Featured Insights* (blog), *McKinsey & Company*, October 8, 2021, https://www.mckinsey.com/featured-insights/mckinsey-on-books/author-talks-indra-nooyi-on-leadership-life-and-crafting-a-better-future.

12. Ibid.

13. Raju Narisetti and Indra Nooyi, "Author Talks: Indra Nooyi on Leadership, Life, and Crafting a Better Future," *Featured Insights* (blog), *McKinsey & Company*, October 8, 2021, https:// www.mckinsey.com/featured-insights/mckinsey-on-books/ author-talks-indra-nooyi-on-leadership-life-and-crafting-a-better-future.

14. Ibid.

15. Raju Narisetti and Indra Nooyi, "Author Talks: Indra Nooyi on Leadership, Life, and Crafting a Better Future," *Featured Insights* (blog), *McKinsey & Company*, October 8, 2021, https:// www.mckinsey.com/featured-insights/mckinsey-on-books/ author-talks-indra-nooyi-on-leadership-life-and-crafting-a-better-future.

16. Tent, "PepsiCo," *Members* (blog), *The Tent Partnership for Refugees*, Accessed January 5, 2024, https://www.tent.org/ partner/pepsico.

17. Sarah Dobson, "Skilled Immigrants Overlooked for Leadership Roles: Report," *HR News* (blog), *Canadian HR Reporter*, March 21, 2016, https://www.hrreporter.com/news/hr-news/skilled-immigrants-overlooked-for-leadership-roles-report/281741.

18. Madeline Zavodny, "NFAP Policy Brief: Why the United States Still Needs Foreign-Born Workers," *NFAP (National Foundation for American Policy)*, July, 2023, https://nfap.com/ research/new-nfap-policy-brief-why-the-united-states-still-needs-foreign-born-workers.

19. Ibid.

20. Madeline Zavodny, "NFAP Policy Brief: Why the United States Still Needs Foreign-Born Workers," *NFAP (National Foundation for American Policy)*, July 2023, https://nfap.com/ research/new-nfap-policy-brief-why-the-united-states-still-needs-foreign-born-workers.

21. Sarah Dobson, "Skilled Immigrants Overlooked for Leadership Roles: Report," *HR News* (blog), *Canadian HR Reporter,* March 21, 2016, https://www.hrreporter.com/news/hr-news/skilled-immigrants-overlooked-for-leadership-roles-report/281741.

22. Ben Horowitz, *The Hard Thing about Hard Things: Building a Business When There Are No Easy Answers* (New York: Harper Business, 2014).

23. Levine, Peter, "What Now: Turning Vision into Execution," *a16z* (blog), *Andreessen Horowitz,* May 11, 2012, https://a16z.com/what-now-turning-vision-into-execution.

CHAPTER 7. INFLUENCE OF IMMIGRANT LEADERSHIP

1. Lynsey Tempest, "How Indra Nooyi Changed the Face of PepsiCo," *Special Reports* (blog), *World Finance,* n.d., https://www.worldfinance.com/special-reports/how-indra-nooyi-changed-the-face-of-pepsico.

2. Ibid.

3. Cheema, Sadia; Akram, Asia; Javed, Farheen, "Employee Engagement and Visionary Leadership: Impact on Customer and Employee Satisfaction," Journal of Business Studies Quarterly; Antioch Vol. 7, Iss. 2, (Dec 2015): 139–148.

4. Danielle Wiener-Bronner, "How Indra Nooyi Built Pepsi for the Future," *CNN Business,* August 7, 2018, https://money.cnn.com/2018/08/07/news/companies/indra-nooyi-legacy/index.html

5. Lynsey Tempest, "How Indra Nooyi Changed the Face of PepsiCo," *Special Reports* (blog), *World Finance,* n.d., https://www.worldfinance.com/special-reports/how-indra-nooyi-changed-the-face-of-pepsico.

6. Kate Taylor, "How Pepsi's CEO predicted the death of soda and saved the beverage giant in the process," *Business Insider,* August 6, 2018, https://www.businessinsider.com/pepsi-ceo-inda-nooyi-predicted-soda-declines-2018-8.

7. Adi Ignatius, "How Indra Nooyi Turned Design Thinking Into Strategy: An Interview with PepsiCo's CEO," *Harvard Business Review*, September, 2015, https://hbr.org/2015/09/how-indra-nooyi-turned-design-thinking-into-strategy.

8. Alice Eagly and Jean Lau Chin, "Diversity and Leadership in a Changing World," *American Psychologist* 65, no. 3 (April 2010): 216–224. https://doi.org/10.1037/a0018957.

9. Inna Lazareva, "How an Immigrant Back Story Builds up Tech Leaders," *Careers* (blog), *CIO*, March 14, 2023, https://www.cio.com/article/463424/how-an-immigrant-back-story-builds-up-tech-leaders.html.

10. Jay A. Conger and Robert M. Fulmer, "Developing Your Leadership Pipeline," *Succession Planning* (blog), *Harvard Business Review*, December 2003, https://hbr.org/2003/12/developing-your-leadership-pipeline.

11. Dame Vivian Hunt, Lareina Yee, Sara Prince, and Sundiatu Dixon-Fyle, "Delivering through diversity" *McKinsey and Company*, January 18, 2018 https://www.mckinsey.com/capabilities/people-and-organizational-performance/our-insights/delivering-through-diversity.

12. Ibid.

13. Dame Vivian Hunt, Lareina Yee, Sara Prince, and Sundiatu Dixon-Fyle, "Delivering through Diversity," *Our Insights* (blog), *McKinsey & Company,* January 18, 2018, https://www.mckinsey.com/capabilities/people-and-organizational-performance/our-insights/delivering-through-diversity.

14. Katina Manko, "Women of Enterprise: Avon and the Women Who Wanted It All," in *Ding Dong! Avon Calling! The Women and Men of Avon Products, Incorporated* (New York: Oxford Academic, 2021), https://doi.org/10.1093/oso/9780190499822.003.0008.

15. Taylor Cox and Stacy Blake, "Managing Cultural Diversity: Implications for Organizational Competitiveness," *The*

Executive 5, no. 3 (August 1991): 45–56, http://www.jstor.org/stable/4165021.

CHAPTER 8. UNDERSTANDING IMMIGRIT

1. Angela Duckworth, "Grit: The Power of Passion and Perseverance," May 9, 2013, TED video and transcript, 00:06:12, https://www.youtube.com/watch?v=H14bBuluwB8.

2. Kelsie Anderson and Aubrey Francisco, "The Research Behind the TED Talk: Angela Duckworth on Grit," *Digital Promise* (blog), updated March 6, 2019, https://digitalpromise.org/2019/03/06/research-behind-ted-talk-angela-duckworth-grit.

3. Helena Seo, "Becoming a Leader as a First-Generation Immigrant," *Engineering Blog* (blog), *DoorDash Engineering*, January 10, 2020, https://doordash.engineering/2020/01/10/becoming-a-leader-as-a-first-generation-immigrant.

4. Nataly Kelly, "Research Shows Immigrants Help Businesses Grow. Here's Why," *Harvard Business Review*, October 26, 2018, https://hbr.org/2018/10/research-shows-immigrants-help-businesses-grow-heres-why.

5. Ben Ramalingam, David Nabarro, Arkebe Oqubay, Dame Ruth Carnall, and Leni Wild, "5 Principles to Guide Adaptive Leadership," *Adaptive Leadership* (blog), *Harvard Business Review*, September 11, 2020, https://hbr.org/2020/09/5-principles-to-guide-adaptive-leadership.

6. Diego Corzo, "Can the American Dream Be Achieved If You Are Not American?" April 2019, TEDxFSU video, 00:12:54, https://www.ted.com/talks/diego_corzo_can_the_american_dream_be_achieved_if_you_are_not_american.

7. Laurence Benenson, "Fact Sheet: Deferred Action for Childhood Arrivals (DACA)," *National Immigration Forum*, October 16, 2020, https://immigrationforum.org/article/fact-sheet-on-deferred-action-for-childhood-arrivals-daca.

8. Kevin Kruse, "The One Trait All Leaders Need, Courtesy of Special Forces," *Leadership Careers* (blog), *Forbes*, August 16, 2017, https://www.forbes.com/sites/kevinkruse/2017/08/16/the-one-trait-all-leaders-need-courtesy-of-special-forces.

9. Rebecca Shi, "The Resilience of Immigrants Is Rebuilding America," *The Catalyst: A Journal of Ideas from the Bush Institute*, no. 21 (Winter 2021), https://www.bushcenter.org/catalyst/state-of-the-american-dream/shi-undocumented-workers-rebuilding-america.

10. Ibid.

11. Sarah Elshahat, Tina Moffat, and K. Bruce Newbold, "Understanding the Healthy Immigrant Effect in the Context of Mental Health Challenges: A Systematic Critical Review," *Journal of Immigrant and Minority Health* 24, no. 6 (December 2022): 1564–1579, https://doi.org/10.1007/s10903-021-01313-5.

12. APA (American Psychological Association), "Building Your Resilience," *Resilience* (blog), *APA*, updated February 1, 2020, https://www.apa.org/topics/resilience/building-your-resilience.

13. Andrea Rice, "What Resilience Is and Isn't," *PsychCentral*, updated January 6, 2022, https://psychcentral.com/lib/what-is-resilience.

14. Margarita Alegría, Kiara Álvarez, and Karissa DiMarzio, "Immigration and Mental Health," *Current Epidemiology Reports* 4, no. 2 (June 2017):145–155, https://doi.org/10.1007/s40471-017-0111-2.

15. CEMS (The Global Alliance in Management Education), *CEMS Guide: Leadership in a Post-COVID-19 World* (Jouy-en-Josas, France: CEMS, 2020), https://cems.app.box.com/s/6f72wtplz476t9sfco7r93ujd52kfiri.

16. Ibid.

17. Ama Marston and Stephanie Marston, *Type R: Transformative Resilience for Thriving in a Turbulent World* (New York: PublicAffairs/Hachette Book Group, 2018).

18. Ibid.

CHAPTER 9. HARNESSING IMMIGRIT

1. Dave Anderson, "Where Did 'the Melting Pot' Come From?" Daveandersonjazz.com, August 15, 2018, https://www.daveandersonjazz.com/blog/2018/8/14/where-did-the-melting-pot-come-from.

2. Laila Lalami, "What Does It Take to 'Assimilate' in America?" *The New York Times*, August 1, 2017, https://www.nytimes.com/2017/08/01/magazine/what-does-it-take-to-assimilate-in-america.html.

3. "About the Episode 'Fiddler: A Miracle of Miracles,'" PBS Great Performances S48 Ep7, November 11, 2020, https://www.pbs.org/wnet/gperf/fiddler-a-miracle-of-miracles-about/12054.

4. Soon Ang and Linn Van Dyne (eds.), *Handbook of Cultural Intelligence: Theory, Measurement, and Applications* (New York: M.E. Sharpe, 2008).

5. Mónica Guzmán, *I Never Thought of It That Way: How to Have Fearlessly Curious Conversations in Dangerously Divided Times* (Dallas, TX: BenBella Books, 2022).

6. Mónica Guzmán, "How Curiosity Will Save Us," November 2021, TEDx video, 00:18:45, https://www.ted.com/talks/monica_guzman_how_curiosity_will_save_us_jan_2022.

CHAPTER 10. CULTIVATING IMMIGRIT

1. Jens Manuel Krogstad and Jynnah Radford, "Education Levels of US Immigrants on the Rise," *High-Skilled Immigration* (blog), *Pew Research Center*, September 14, 2018, https://www.pewresearch.org/short-reads/2018/09/14/education-levels-of-u-s-immigrants-are-on-the-rise.

2. Sarah Bohn and Eric Schiff, "Immigrants and the Labor Market," *Fact Sheet* (blog), *Public Policy Institute of California*, March 2011, https://www.ppic.org/publication/immigrants-and-the-labor-market.

3. Barry Chiswick, "Immigrants in the US Labor Market," *The ANNALS of the American Academy of Political and Social Science* 460, no. 1 (March, 1982): 64–72, https://doi.org/10.1177/00027 16282460001008.

4. Harvey J. Coleman, *Type R: Empowering Yourself: The Organizational Game Revealed* (Kendall/Hunt Pub., 1996).

5. The Networking Institute, "The PIE Theory: Performance, Image, and Exposure in Career Progression," *The Networking Institute,* July 21, 2023, https://thenetworkinginstitute.com/media/networking/the-pie-theory-performance-image-and-exposure-in-career-progression.

6. Scott Stump, "Most NFL Players Are Black. So Why Aren't There More Black Head Coaches?" *NBC News*, September 15, 2020, https://www.nbcnews.com/news/nbcblk/most-nfl-players-are-black-so-why-aren-t-there-n1240131.

7. David Thomas, "The Truth About Mentoring Minorities: Race Matters," *Harvard Business Review* 79, no. 4 (April 2001), https://hbr.org/2001/04/race-matters.

8. Alison Beard and Sylvia Ann Hewlett, "The Surprising Benefits of Sponsoring Others at Work," *HBR IdeaCast,* April 8, 2020, 0026:06, https://hbr.org/podcast/2019/06/the-surprising-benefits-of-sponsoring-others-at-work.

9. Sami Mahroum and Rashid Ansari, "What the Data Tells Us about Immigrant Executives in the US," *Consumer Behavior* (blog), *Harvard Business Review*, August 31, 2021, https://hbr.org/2017/11/what-the-data-tells-us-about-immigrant-executives-in-the-u-s.

1. Higher Ed Immigration Portal, "National Data on Immigrant Students," *Presidents' Alliance on Higher Education and Immigration*, accessed November 13, 2023, https://www.higheredimmigrationportal.org/national/national-data.

2. Ibid.

3. Higher Ed Immigration Portal, "National Data on Immigrant Students," *Presidents' Alliance on Higher Education and Immigration*, accessed November 13, 2023, https://www.higheredimmigrationportal.org/national/national-data.

4. Ibid.

5. Nichole Argo, PhD and Hammad Sheikh, PhD, "The Belonging Barometer: The State of Belonging in America," *American Immigration Council*, March 7, 2023 https://www.americanimmigrationcouncil.org/sites/default/files/research/the_belonging_barometer_-_the_state_of_belonging_in_america.pdf.

6. Ibid.

7. Nichole Argo, PhD and Hammad Sheikh, PhD, "The Belonging Barometer: The State of Belonging in America" *American Immigration Council,* March 7, 2023, https://www.americanimmigrationcouncil.org/sites/default/files/research/the_belonging_barometer_-_the_state_of_belonging_in_america.pdf.

8. Charles Duhigg, "What Google Learned from Its Quest to Build the Perfect Team," *The New York Times*, February 25, 2016, https://www.nytimes.com/2016/02/28/magazine/what-google-learned-from-its-quest-to-build-the-perfect-team.html.

9. DiversityInc Staff, "Exploring the History and Evolution of Employee Resource Groups," *Talent Programs* (blog), *Fair360*, August 5, 2020, https://www.fair360.com/history-and-evolution-of-employee-resource-groups-ergs-2.

10. Stephanie Jensen "ERGs engage employees and drive better business in the Triangle" *Triangle Business Journal*, Sep 15, 2021 https://www.bizjournals.com/triangle/news/2021/09/15/ergs-engage-employees-and-drive-better-business.html.

11. Natacha Catalino, Nora Gardner, Drew Goldstein, and Jackie Wong, "Effective Employee Resource Groups Are Key to Inclusion at Work. Here's How to Get Them Right," McKinsey & Company, December 7, 2022, https://www.mckinsey.com/capabilities/people-and-organizational-performance/our-insights/effective-employee-resource-groups-are-key-to-inclusion-at-work-heres-how-to-get-them-right.

12. Sarah Jackson, "Workers All Over the World Have Hit a New Record for Stress on the Job—And That's Not Even the Worst of It," *Business Insider*, June 16, 2022, https://www.businessinsider.com/workers-were-more-stressed-than-ever-last-year-gallup-report-2022-6.

13. Jamie Stein, "Employee Mental Health Issues Intensify," *ComPsych,* November 3, 2021, https://www.compsych.com/press-room/press-article?nodeId=009fcce1-bf27-4ce7-8d20-1d86508f2e03.

14. Jamie Stein, "Mental Health Support Is Top Concern for Both Employers and Employees," *Business Wire*, April 20, 2022, https://www.businesswire.com/news/home/20220420005814/en/Mental-Health-Support-Is-Top-Concern-for-Both-Employers-and-Employees.

15. Tené Lewis, Courtney Cogburn, and David Williams, "Self-Reported Experiences of Discrimination and Health: Scientific Advances, Ongoing Controversies, and Emerging Issues," *Annual Review of Clinical Psychology* 11 (March 2015): 407–440. https://doi.org/10.1146/annurev-clinpsy-032814-112728.

16. Amelia Seraphia Derr, "Mental Health Service Use Among Immigrants in the United States: Systematic Review," *Psychiatric Services*, Vol 67 Issue 3 (March 01, 2016), 265–274, https://doi.org/10.1176/appi.ps.201500004.

17. Monique Verduyn, "What Is an Employee Assistance Program (EAP)? Your In-depth 2024 Guide," *Academy of Innovate HR* (blog), https://www.aihr.com/blog/employee-assistance-program-eap.

18. Ibid.

19. Monique Verduyn, "What Is an Employee Assistance Program (EAP)? Your In-depth 2024 Guide," *Academy of Innovate HR* (blog), https://www.aihr.com/blog/employee-assistance-program-eap.

20. Ibid.

21. Cone Communications, "Americans Willing to Buy or Boycott Companies Based on Corporate Values, According to New Research by Cone Communications," *PR News Wire*, May 17, 2017, https://www.prnewswire.com/news-releases/americans-willing-to-buy-or-boycott-companies-based-on-corporate-values-according-to-new-research-by-cone-communications-300459220.html.

22. Tim Stobierski, "15 Eye-Opening Corporate Social Responsibility Statistics," *Harvard Business School Online*, June 15, 2021, https://online.hbs.edu/blog/post/corporate-social-responsibility-statistics.

23. Kathy Gurchiek, "Report: CSR Is On the Rise, But the Motivation for It Has Changed" SHRM December 5, 2023, https://www.shrm.org/topics-tools/news/report-csr-is-on-the-rise-but-the-motivation-for-it-has-changed.

24. The Associated Press, "CEOs Push Back against Trump Temporary Immigration Ban," *The Denver Post,* January 30, 2017, https://www.denverpost.com/2017/01/30/ceos-push-back-against-trump-travel-ban.

PARTING WORDS

1. Dennis Gabor, *Inventing the Future* (London: Secker & Warburg, 1963).

2. Shivbhadrasinh Gohil, "WhatsApp Statistics 2024—Usage, Users, Revenue & More," *Ecommerce* (blog), *Meetanshi Blog*, n.d., https://meetanshi.com/blog/whatsapp-statistics.

3. Johann Daniel Harnoss, "How Your Company Can Gain a Global Talent Advantage," July 2023, TED video and transcript, 00:11:40, https://www.ted.com/talks/johann_daniel_harnoss_how_your_company_can_gain_a_global_talent_advantage?language=en.

4. Johann Harnoss, Janina Kugel, Karina Kleissl, Marley Finley, and François Candelon, *Migration Matters: A Human Cause with a $20 Trillion Business Case* (Boston, MA: Boston Consulting Group, 2022), https://web-assets.bcg.com/1a/d1/ed3e7b194e0599500062157of19d2/bcg-migration-matters-a-human-cause-with-a-20-trillion-business-dec-2022-3.pdf.

5. Ibid.

6. Johann Harnoss, Janina Kugel, Karina Kleissl, Marley Finley, and François Candelon, *Migration Matters: A Human Cause with a $20 Trillion Business Case* (Boston, MA: Boston Consulting Group, 2022), https://web-assets.bcg.com/1a/d1/ed3e7b194e0599500062157of19d2/bcg-migration-matters-a-human-cause-with-a-20-trillion-business-dec-2022-3.pdf.

7a. Kate Whiting, "These Are the Top 10 Job Skills of Tomorrow—And How Long It Takes to Learn Them," *Education* (blog), *World Economic Forum*, October 21, 2020, https://www.weforum.org/agenda/2020/10/top-10-work-skills-of-tomorrow-how-long-it-takes-to-learn-them.

7b. Jo Taylor, "Resilience and Adaptability Are Key to Navigating Today's World. Here's Why," *Business* (blog), *World Economic Forum*, January 14, 2024, https://www.weforum.org/agenda/2024/01/resilience-adaptability-key-navigating.

8. Julia Gelatt, Jeanne Batalova, and Randy Capps, "Navigating the Future of Work: The Role of Immigrant-Origin Workers in the Changing US," *Research* (blog), *Migration Policy Institute*,

October, 2020, https://www.migrationpolicy.org/research/future-work-immigrant-origin-workers-us-economy.

9. Ibid.

10. Yannick Binvel, Michael Franzino, Alan Guarino, Werner Penk and Jean-Marc Laouchez, "The $8.5 Trillion Talent Shortage," *This Week in Leadership* (blog), *Korn Ferry*, July 26, 2021, https://www.kornferry.com/insights/this-week-in-leadership/talent-crunch-future-of-work.

11. Ibid.

12. Anthony Knapp and Tiangeng Lu, "Net Migration between the United States and Abroad in 2022 Reaches Highest Level Since 2017," *America Counts: Stories* (blog), *United States Census Bureau*, December 22, 2022, https://www.census.gov/library/stories/2022/12/net-international-migration-returns-to-pre-pandemic-levels.html.

13. Ibid.

WHAT'S NEXT?

IT'S TIME TO UNLEASH IMMIGRIT!
By now, you should feel better equipped to navigate disruption, drive innovation, and deliver outsized business growth by leveraging global talent. Through the strategies in this book, you have the tools to foster cultural competence, conduct curious conversations, and create an environment where IMMIGRIT thrives. So, how do you get others to come along on the journey with you?

Here are three ways to get started:

- **Copies for your team:** Buy copies of *IMMIGRIT* for your team and I'll send you a free slide presentation you can use to facilitate a group discussion

- **Copies for your whole organization:** Contact me about discounted bulk purchases and special offers so you can purchase this book for everyone at your company, organization, community or conference hello@ immigritbook.com

- **Speaking at your event.** Are you looking for an engaging speaker? Think of me when you are coordinating your next conference, team offsite or retreat.

LET'S START THE CONVERSATION

Send me an email or reach out on social to discuss these options for your team and organization. I can't wait to hear from you!

✉ contact@ukstopia.com

🛑 www.ukstopia.com

in linkedin.com/in/ukstopia

📷 Instagram.com/ukstopia

THANK YOU FOR READING!

If you enjoyed IMMIGRIT please leave a review at Goodreads or on the retail site where you purchased this book and help me reach more readers like you.

9 798889 260653